QuickBooks® in One Hour
FOR LAWYERS

LYNETTE BENTON

ABA LAW
PRACTICE
DIVISION
The Business of Practicing Law

17 16 15 14 13   5 4 3 2 1

Library of Congress Cataloging-in-Publication Data

Benton, Lynette, author.
  Quickbooks in one hour for lawyers / by Lynette Benton.
    pages cm
  Includes bibliographical references.
  ISBN 978-1-62722-161-0
  1. Lawyers—United States—Accounting. 2. Law offices—United States—Automation. 3. QuickBooks.
I. American Bar Association. Section of Law Practice Management, sponsoring body. II. Title.
  KF320.A2B46 2013
  657'.834—dc23

                                                                    2013041851

Contents

About the Author

Lynette Benton has been a QuickBooks certified ProAdvisor since QuickBooks started the program in 1999. As the President of Computer Technology Services, a technology and consulting firm in North Florida, Lynette specializes in teaching and training lawyers and law firms to use QuickBooks. She has set up and trained hundreds of lawyers and small law firms on how to use QuickBooks efficiently in their law practices. She works as a consultant and has designed custom manuals for several state bar associations, including the Florida Bar.

Known as the QuickBooks expert in the industry, Lynette has consulted with Intuit (http://www.intuit.com) and has written some of the help files for past versions of QuickBooks Premier Professional Services edition.

She has written several books including *Trust Accounting Using QuickBooks*, *Law Practice Accounting Using QuickBooks,* and *Law Practice Accounting Using QuickBooks for MAC*, all of which are available from her website at www.attorneystechnology.com. She works with clients both local and remote and is available for remote online training and technology consulting services.

Born in Silicon Valley, Lynette now lives in Fleming Island, Florida, and is a wife and mother of two children. Lynette loves to teach and work with business owners and professionals. If you know her, you are familiar with the phrases "No worries" and *"Yippee"* often heard coming from her office.

Dedication

I would like to dedicate this book to one of my first clients, Mr. James Keenan. Many years ago, he asked me to come to his office and show him how to use QuickBooks in his law practice. All he wanted to do was track his income and expenses. Having some experience with QuickBooks, I agreed, and while I was working with him I created a self-help document he could use when I was not around. After several visits he stopped me and told me that I should write a book, because he knew he was not the only one having trouble figuring out how to use QuickBooks. Thank you Mr. Keenan, for your guidance and being my test subject. Your support has helped change my life and my career. I am eternally grateful.

I also want to take a moment to thank my husband Randy, who was instrumental in me writing my first book. He would describe himself as Mr. Awesome and I would have to agree, at least some of the time. ;) Randy encouraged me to take the time to sit down and write that first draft. He has been there all along as a friend, colleague, sounding board, brainstorming partner, and shoulder to lean on. His patience and support are what gave me the confidence I needed to succeed. I am so lucky to have such a wonderful companion and friend.

Preface

QuickBooks (http://quickbooks.intuit.com/) is a very popular accounting software package. Many small and medium-sized businesses use it every day for all of their accounting needs. It is inexpensive and easy to use, especially when compared to the full accounting packages used by large corporations and law firms. However, many lawyers are under the impression that QuickBooks is not suitable for their needs because it is not made specifically for lawyers. They also think they cannot track and bill their clients for time, or create professional looking invoices and statements. Having worked with hundreds of law firms over the last fifteen years, I can tell you that this is just not true.

QuickBooks has many more features than you will ever use, but all of the basic accounting tools you will need in your law practice are there; once you get the hang of the terminology and the processes, you will see that QuickBooks will do all that you want and more. QuickBooks can be used in a law firm, and I am going to show you how easy it is.

Let's take a quick inventory of what every law firm needs in an accounting software package:

- You need a way to track your income and expenses.
- You need a way to track and bill your clients for time and expenses and see how much your clients owe you.
- You need a way to send out monthly statements to remind your clients they owe you money.
- You might need others in the office to access the program to enter time or expenses, and you need the ability to control what they can

see. (Your timekeepers don't usually need access to your check register or profit-and-loss reports, and you might want to block them from accessing sensitive financial information.)

- You may also need a way to track escrow or trust-account payments received from clients, and expenses paid on their behalf. This is important because you must be able to provide necessary reports to be in compliance with bar regulations.

QuickBooks can handle all of this and much more. Here are a few of the features that QuickBooks has to offer:

Expenses. You have the ability to record expenses through the check register and the credit card register. QuickBooks can also track the expenses that will be billed to clients.

Time Tracking. QuickBooks includes a timer to track time and record billable and non-billable time spent on clients and administrative work.

Billing. You can use QuickBooks to create invoices from time and expenses, as well as for flat fee work you do.

Accounts Receivable. By processing your billing with QuickBooks, you have the ability to receive payments from clients and keep track of who owes you money.

Multi-User. When you purchase additional copies, QuickBooks allows you to store the data file on a server or shared folder so you can have multiple people use the program simultaneously. You can set up users and define what they have the ability to see in QuickBooks, keeping select (sensitive) information confidential.

Payroll. QuickBooks has a great add-on payroll service in which you can choose to create payroll in house, have your accountant process quarterly returns, or if you choose the Full Service Payroll, QuickBooks will do all your tax depositing and report filing for you.

Financial Reporting. When you process all your income and expenses through QuickBooks, you will have the ability to create financial statements and keep track of how your law practice is doing during any given period. Using QuickBooks, you can instantly generate profit-and-loss reports, balance-sheet reports, and many other reports—they're all built into the program.

Trust Accounting. QuickBooks can handle your trust-accounting transactions and give you the reports you need to stay in compliance with trust accounting regulations.

Law firms are like people; no two are exactly alike. We have a way of doing things that work best for us and our businesses. While we all follow the same basic accounting principles, the software that we choose must be flexible and easy to use so it can adapt to our needs. One of the downfalls of accounting packages attached to big practice-management programs is that they require you to spend hours and hours in training courses to figure out how to accomplish simple tasks; you almost have to be certified in the software. That's what makes QuickBooks great. The software designers have made the software in such a way that if you just look at the screen, you can probably figure out how to do the task. Once you get the basics down, QuickBooks really is a great program. With that said, a little training and a review of this book can help you feel confident in your ability to handle your financial transactions in QuickBooks and get the reports you need to see how your business is doing.

NOTE: QuickBooks offers different versions of the product: Professional Services, Premier, Pro, and many more. Each version offers a different set of features. Choosing the correct version for your needs is important, so please see Appendix A, Which Version of QuickBooks Do You Choose?, to learn more about the differences and how to pick the right version.

My goal for this book is to cover the basics of QuickBooks and show you some of the features you will use in your law firm. This book is not intended as a comprehensive guide to everything you can do with Quick-Books, but more of a guide to getting started. Once you master the basic features, you may want to dig a little deeper and learn more about the other features available. There are many resources to help you do this—print books and online training and videos, including resources at my website, AttorneysTechnology.com.

QuickBooks can handle all of your time-tracking, billing, expenses, payroll, and other accounting features you need for your law firm, but don't just take my word for it. Let's get started and I will show you first-hand the ins and outs of using QuickBooks in your law practice.

Getting Started

Before we can begin, you need to purchase QuickBooks and get it installed on your computer. Installation is easy, with a few standard software install screens. Just select the recommended settings, and you should not have any issues at all. During the install process, you will need to enter your license keys, and once the process is complete, you will need to register your copy online. QuickBooks will remind you that you need to register, and it will limit the number of times that you can use it until it is fully registered.

Creating Your Company File

Once QuickBooks is installed on your computer, and before we can go any further, we must create a Company File. This is the file QuickBooks uses to store all of your information. By default, QuickBooks stores this company file in a public shared folder on your computer. However, if you are going to have multiple users of QuickBooks you can store the file on a server or other shared folder.

> **NOTE:** If multiple computers will access one data file, it is important that you read the installation instructions carefully. QuickBooks calls this a multi-user environment.

When you open QuickBooks for the first time, you are likely to see a screen similar to Figure 1.1.

Figure 1.1 Set-Up Screen

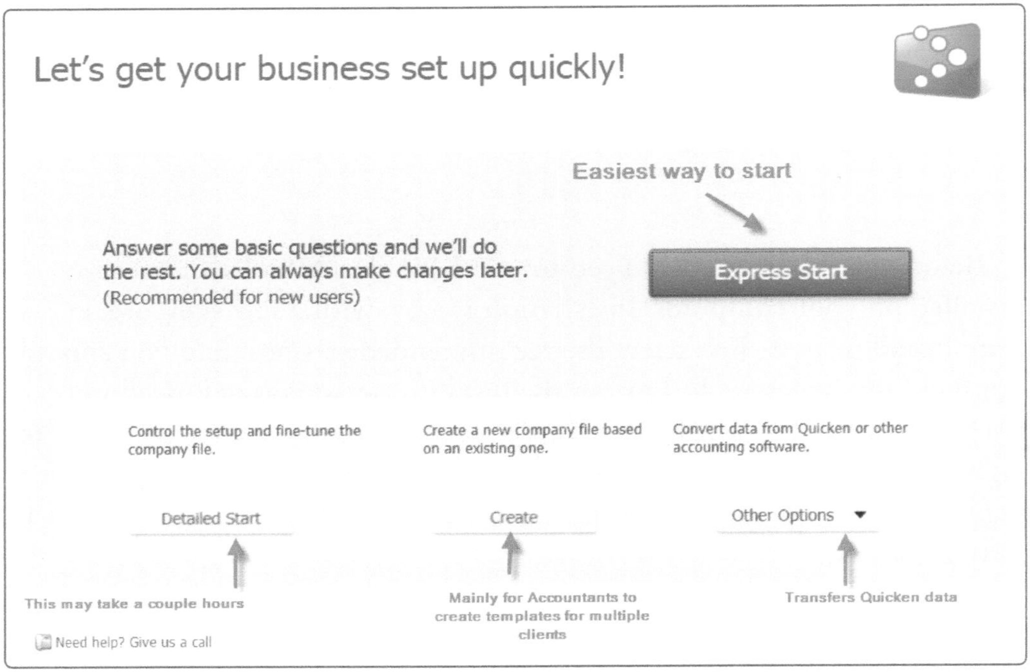

Let's get your business set up quickly!

Easiest way to start

Answer some basic questions and we'll do the rest. You can always make changes later. (Recommended for new users)

Express Start

Control the setup and fine-tune the company file.

Create a new company file based on an existing one.

Convert data from Quicken or other accounting software.

Detailed Start

Create

Other Options ▼

This may take a couple hours

Mainly for Accountants to create templates for multiple clients

Transfers Quicken data

Need help? Give us a call

You will see a few options to choose from. If you choose the **Detailed Start** button, you can walk through the setup wizard to create your company file. *I don't recommend this option* because it will take a considerable amount of time to complete (several hours), and you need to have everything right at your fingertips. The **Create** button will create a company file based on an existing company file, and this option is mainly for accountants who have set up templates for their clients. The **Other Options** button is what you would use if you want to convert data from other accounting software or a Quicken data file.

For a lawyer who is using QuickBooks for the first time, the easiest way to get started is the **Express Start** option, so that is what we will use for our example. This option will set up your company file based on the industry you choose. In our case, we will choose Legal Services. I have included a Setup Checklist in Appendix B that you can use as a guide to gathering information you may need.

Click the *Express Start* button to begin.

Fill in the basic information about the type of company you have and click the *Continue* button to advance to the next screen (see Figure 1.2).

Figure 1.2 Entering Basic Information

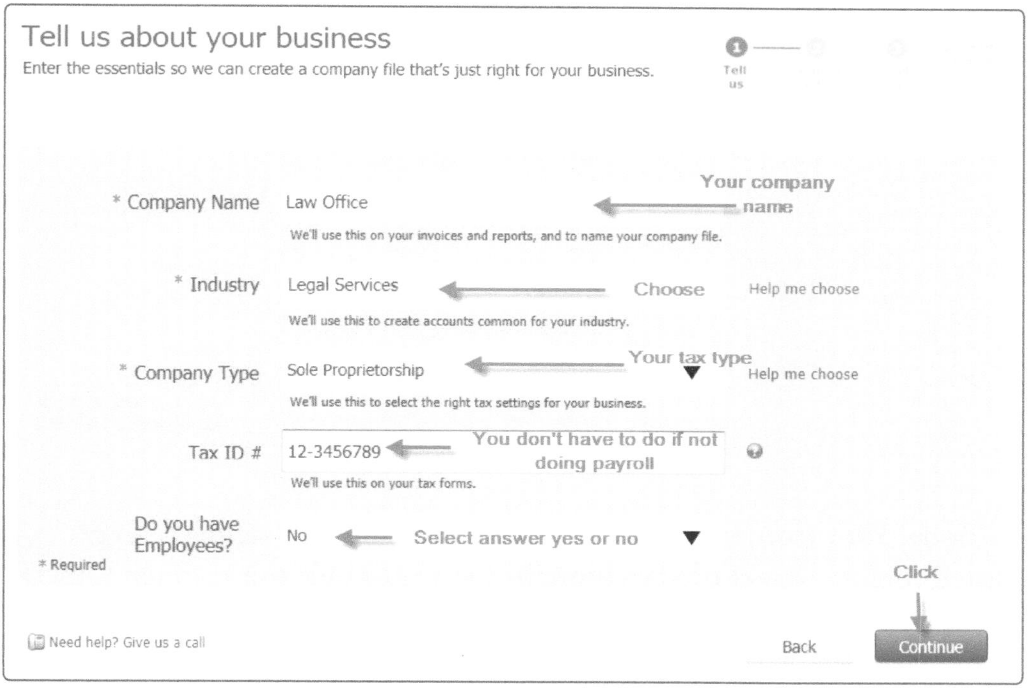

Tell us about your business
Enter the essentials so we can create a company file that's just right for your business.

* Company Name	Law Office	← Your company name
	We'll use this on your invoices and reports, and to name your company file.	
* Industry	Legal Services	← Choose Help me choose
	We'll use this to create accounts common for your industry.	
* Company Type	Sole Proprietorship	← Your tax type ▼ Help me choose
	We'll use this to select the right tax settings for your business.	
Tax ID #	12-3456789	← You don't have to do if not doing payroll
	We'll use this on your tax forms.	
Do you have Employees?	No	← Select answer yes or no ▼

* Required

Click ↓ Continue

Need help? Give us a call   Back   Continue

Next, fill in your address and contact information (see Figure 1.3). While you do not have to fill in all the fields, doing more now will save you some time down the road.

When you are finished, click the ***Create Company File*** button.

Figure 1.3 Entering Contact Information

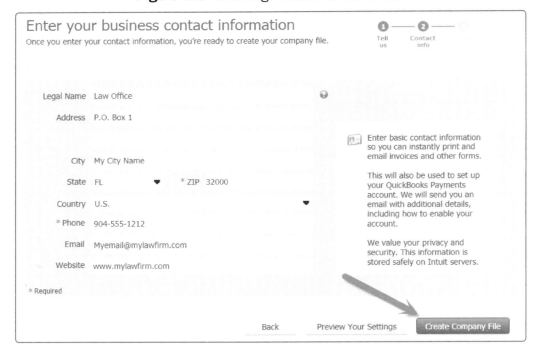

Ta-da! Your Company Data File is created, and you are ready to get started. Before we get too far, though, I want to walk you through Quick-Books' main screen and different ways to navigate the program.

Getting Around

Once you create the file, it should open, and you should see a window similar to Figure 1.4.

This is your **Home Page**. If you don't see this, click *Company* from the Main Menu at the top, then click *Home Page*.

Figure 1.4 Home Page

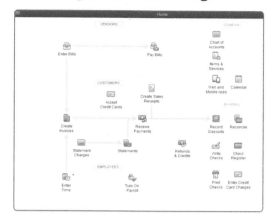

NOTE: Your Home Page may look a little different depending on the version of QuickBooks you have. If yours does not look exactly like Figure 1.4, don't worry. The basic processes that we are going to cover work in all PC versions of the software, unless I note otherwise.

The Home Page is your base for navigating the program. As Figure 1.5 shows, it is organized into sections by types of activities, and it is arranged like a map that shows the flow of information inside the program. Let's take a brief look at the different sections on the Home Page.

Figure 1.5 Home Page Sections

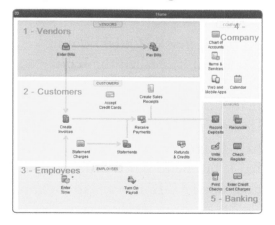

1. **Vendors.** At the top center is the Vendors section where you can enter bills, pay bills, or access your vendor list.

2. **Customers.** Below Vendors is the Customers area. Here you can access your customer (client) list, create bills, create statements, and receive payments from clients.

3. **Employees.** The section at bottom center is the Employees section, where you can access your employee information, enter time, and turn on the payroll feature if you wish to use QuickBooks for payroll operations.

4. **Company.** Next, at the top right, is the Company section. This is where you can access your company chart of accounts, and the item lists that you will use for time tracking and billing.

5. **Banking.** Below Company is the Banking section. This is where you can make deposits, use your check register, write checks, and reconcile your bank account.

On the left side of your screen, next to the Home Page, is a grey area with different options (see Figure 1.6).

This is new to QuickBooks 2013, and it is called the **Icon Bar**. It is filled with shortcuts that you can use to access different features of the program. I have found that when the Icon

Figure 1.6 Icon Bar

Bar is on the top, it is easier to use because it takes up less space on the desktop view. To move it to the top, find the Main Menu across the top of

the window, and click **View**. Select ***Top Icon Bar***, as shown in Figure 1.7.

Figure 1.7
Moving the Icon Bar

When you move the Icon Bar you will notice it is prefilled with shortcuts (see Figure 1.8). The nice thing about the Icon Bar is that you can customize it with your own shortcuts.

Figure 1.8 Icon Bar at the Top of the Screen

I recommend customizing the Icon Bar to suit your needs once you get used to using QuickBooks and you have a better idea of the features you use the most. To customize the Icon Bar, click ***View*** in the Main Menu and select ***Customize Icon Bar.***

Figure 1.9 Customize the Icon Bar by Deleting

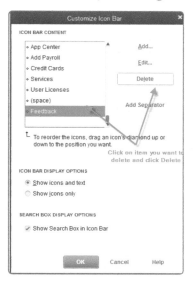

Figure 1.9 shows a window that displays the different options available. Here you can delete some of the icons and add some that you frequently use. When you delete something from the Icon Bar, it is not the same as deleting it completely. It's just deleting the shortcut from the Icon Bar. Let's delete Feedback for practice. Click ***Feedback*** and then click the ***Delete*** button.

Now let's add the Find Transactions icon. Click the ***Add*** button and a window will appear that lets you add the features you use the most (see Figure 1.10a). Scroll down the left side to find the feature and then type in a name for it on the right. Click ***Ok*** when done.

Figure 1.10a Customize the Icon Bar by Adding Shortcuts

Now you will see in Figure 1.10b that the toolbar has a shortcut to find transactions.

Figure 1.10b Customize the Icon Bar: Icon Added

Finally, take a look at the Main Menu bar at the top of the screen. See Figure 1.11. The Main Menu gives you access to all the features in Quick-Books. Click *Lists* from the Main Menu. You will see all the things you can do with Lists.

Figure 1.11 Lists Options

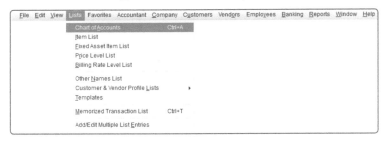

Throughout the book I will reference the Home Page, Main Menu, and Icon Bar. In almost all cases, you will see that there are several ways to get to the same feature through one of these areas. For example, let's say you want to get to the Customers. There is an icon on the Home Page and on the Icon Bar, and you can always find your Customers on the Main Menu by clicking *Customers*. There is no right or wrong way as long as you get where you need to go.

Now that we have the basics down on the layout of the program, let's get the accounting language down by going over the terms QuickBooks uses and how they relate to your law firm.

QuickBooks Terms

QuickBooks uses terms that may be new to you. They are mainly accounting terms you may not have heard since that semester of accounting in college. Below are a listing and a brief description of the QuickBooks terms we use in this book, and what they mean.

- **Chart of Accounts.** This is a listing of accounts or categories that form the income and expenses you have in your company.
- **Class.** You will use a Class to create departments or locations. For example, you might have offices in multiple locations, one located in Jacksonville and one in Orlando. By using Classes, you can separate the income and expenses for each office location to see the separate profitability of each office.
- **Vendors.** These are people you buy from or pay for services, like the Clerk of the Court, the Postal Service, or the office supply store.
- **Customers.** These are your clients.

- **Jobs.** These are different cases or matters you have with a particular client.

- **Items & Services.** You may be familiar with the term **billing code**. Items are very similar to billing codes. They are a listing of different services or time activities for which you bill your clients. You use Items when you are tracking time and creating invoices. Examples of Items include Legal Fees, Paralegal Services, and Postage or copying charges.

Our next step is to customize our Company Data File so we can turn on/off some options that QuickBooks sets by default. You should find this helpful and we will do it through setting preferences.

Setting Preferences

QuickBooks allows you to set your own particular preferences to help you better use the program. There are many preferences that can be set and changed; the following are the basic preferences that I feel you should change from the default settings. This will allow you to navigate the program more easily and activate some features not already activated by default.

To get started, click *Edit* from the Main Menu and choose *Preferences*.

On the left side of the window you will see categories, and on the right you will see the preferences available for that category (see Figure 1.12). Let's review some of the options.

Figure 1.12 General: My Preferences

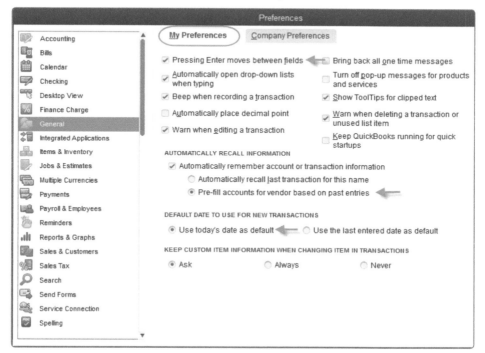

General

This preferences option is in the left pane. In the middle of the main window, at the top there are two tabs; one is **My Preferences** and the other is **Company Preferences**. My Preferences changes things just for you—the user that is logged in. Company Preferences are universal changes made by the administrator for all users and cannot be changed by individual users.

Click the *My Preferences* tab. Figure 1.12 shows some of the settings that you, as an individual user, might want to change. Here you can configure the way in which some functions and keys work in QuickBooks.

- **Pressing Enter moves between fields**. Check this preference box because if you leave it unchecked, then the Enter button is the save-and-new button. When you accidently press the Enter button it will save the transaction you were on and take you to a new transaction even if you are not finished with the transaction you are currently working on.

- **Automatically remember account or transaction information.** Check the preference box labeled **Pre-fill accounts for vendors based on past entries** because it will pre-fill the expense accounts used for that vendor which helps you maintain consistency. For example, when you enter a check for a purchase from the office supply store, it will pre-fill the account you used to expense purchases with this vendor based on the last time it was used. If the last time you coded an expense from the Office supply store was to Office supplies, then Office supplies will come up automatically for you when you choose this vendor the next time.

- **Use today's date as default**. You probably want to check this preference box so that all new transactions created will be dated today's date by default. You can change the date if you need to. However, if you are adding a lot of historical data, you may want to use the other option, **Use the last entered date as default.**

Now Click the ***Company Preferences*** tab. These options can only be set by the company administrator, but since we just got started and have not set up any users yet, you are the company administrator. Figure 1.13, shows the option for Time Format. This is for your time tracking. **Decimal** works best with the time entries on timesheets because it allows you to enter time in tenths of an hour. When you use the **Minutes** format, QuickBooks adjusts the time entries, and it can become confusing.

Figure 1.13 General: Company Preferences

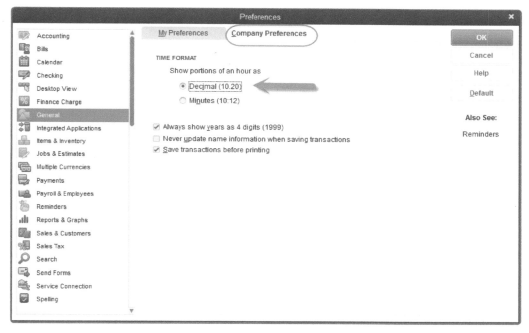

Below are a few more preferences I would recommend that you review before starting to use the program.

Desktop View

From the left pane choose *Desktop View*. On the **My Preferences** tab you can change to show **One Window** or **Multiple Windows** (see Figure 1.14). I think you will like the Multiple Windows option best because it allows you to see multiple reports at one time. This is very helpful when we get into billing clients later in the lessons.

- **Company File Color Scheme.** Towards the bottom of the screen you will see an option to change the color scheme. If you do not like the default color scheme that QuickBooks uses, just pick one from the drop down list.

Figure 1.14 Desktop View

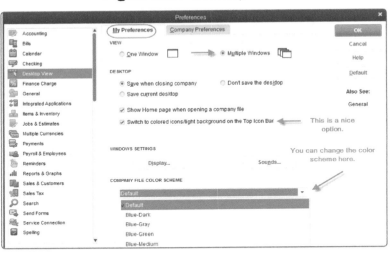

- The **Company Preferences** tab for Desktop View allows the administrator to turn on and off some of the icons that appear on all users' Home Pages. Turn off features that you will not be using, so your Home Page will not be cluttered with these icons. The administrator can turn them back on at any time.

Figure 1.15 Estimates, Sales Orders, and Payroll

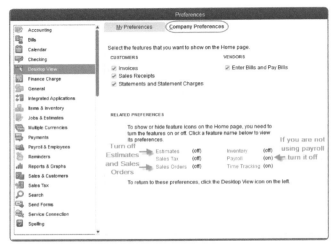

- **Estimates** and **Sales Orders** are not generally used in a law firm, so I would turn these off. When you turn off a feature you may see a window pop up that says QuickBooks must close all windows. This is fine, and you should let QuickBooks close them. You will then have to go back to Edit and Preferences from the Main Menu to continue setting Preferences (see Figure 1.15).

- If you are not planning to use **Payroll** in QuickBooks, turn it off.

Sales & Customers

Click this option in the left panel. Then click the *My Preferences* tab to see an option labeled **Prompt for time/costs to add** (see Figure 1.16). Leave this selected because it will remind you to look at expenses and time that may be billable when you are invoicing a client.

Figure 1.16 Prompt for Time/Costs to Add

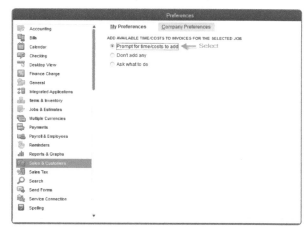

On the **Company Preferences** tab (see Figure 1.17) you can turn off **Enable Sales Orders** because you won't be using these. If you have the Premier edition, select *Use price levels*. I will show you in Lesson 5 how to use this fantastic feature.

Figure 1.17 Sales Orders and Price Levels (Premier Edition)

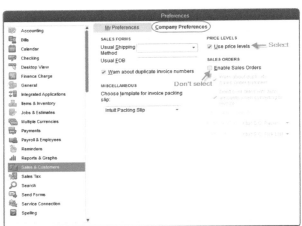

Reports & Graphs

Click *Reports & Graphs* in the left panel. In the **My Preferences** tab is an option to **Refresh automatically** (see Figure 1.18). This will allow any open report to update automatically after you change a transaction. This is a great feature, so make sure it is selected.

Figure 1.18 Reports & Graphs

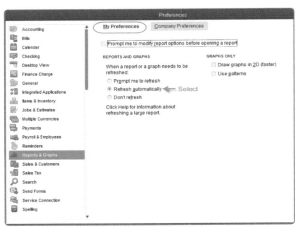

In the **Company Preferences** tab, the administrator can set the defaults for reports (see Figure 1.19).

- **Cash- or Accrual- Basis Accounting.** The most common method of accounting for a law office is cash-basis accounting. This is reporting income based on the cash you actually received, not the amount you have billed that is still outstanding.

Figure 1.19 Reports & Graphs: Company Preferences

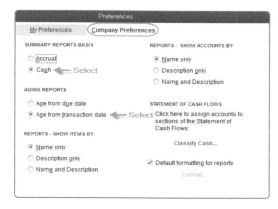

- **Aging Reports.** When you do billing in QuickBooks, you will have the ability to create aging reports on balances due to you by your clients. If your terms are due upon receipt, you may want to consider using **Age from transaction date**. If you choose the **Age from due date**, you will need to set up your clients with terms, and this will then create the reports based on the due date for the transactions.

Accounting

Click *Accounting* in the left panel. In the My Preferences tab you will see **Autofill memo in the journal entry** (see Figure 1.20). This is a useful feature because when you are creating journal entries, it will copy the description or memo about the entry to each line.

Figure 1.20 Autofill Memo in the Journal Entry

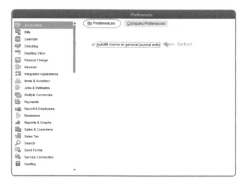

In the Company Preferences tab (Figure 1.21) the administrator will see other options, such as **Use account numbers**, **Class**, **Date Warnings**, and **Closing Date**.

Figure 1.21 Accounting: Company Preferences

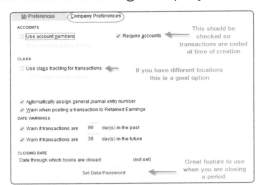

- **Use account numbers**. Lesson 2 describes how you can set up and modify your chart of accounts, which is a listing of categories you put your income and expenses into. For example, Office supplies, Rent, Travel, and Utilities are accounts to which you will code expenses. You may have a tax professional who recommends that you use his or her chart of accounts, and your tax advisor may also request that you use account numbers. Here is where you can set up your chart of accounts with numbers and descriptions. Using account numbers is not necessary, and I would not use this feature unless your accountant wants you to.

- **Use class tracking for transactions.** If you have multiple locations, use this option to track your income and expense from each location. You can also use this feature if you have a partner or partners in the firm and you want to track income and expense by partners.

- **Closing Date**. This is a feature best used when you are finished with an accounting period, such as at year end when you have given your information to your tax preparer. I recommend setting the closing date for that period so you don't accidently change that information.

Send Forms

Click this option in the left panel. QuickBooks has the ability to e-mail Invoices, Paystubs, and Reports from within QuickBooks. In My Preferences (see Figure 1.22) there are options for choosing how to e-mail. You can e-mail directly from QuickBooks using Outlook, Outlook Express, Thunderbird, or major web mail services (such as Yahoo or Gmail), and if you subscribe to one of the advanced QuickBooks services such as payroll or merchant services, you can also use the **QuickBooks Email** service. Most users will select the **Web Mail** option.

> **NOTE:** When you e-mail a form from QuickBooks, it will create a PDF to add to an e-mail as an attachment. People that you send the forms to will need a PDF reader installed on their computer (like Adobe Reader [get.adobe.com/reader/]) to view the forms. PDF readers are free and included on most computers, but you can also include a link in your default message to download a free PDF reader when you e-mail your clients.

Figure 1.22 E-mail from QuickBooks

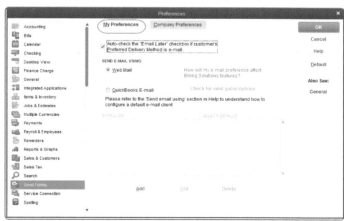

The Company Preferences tab lets the administrator set up a default e-mail message that can be used when sending forms: choose the form and configure the default message that will appear for that type of form. You can always customize the message before sending an e-mail, but setting up the general language can save time when you are sending out forms to multiple people in one sitting (see Figure 1.23).

Figure 1.23 Company Preferences

Time & Expenses

Click this option in the left panel. There is no My Preferences tab for this. Click the ***Company Preferences*** tab to set the defaults for time tracking (see Figure 1.24).

- **First Day of the Work Week.** Here you can change the first day of the week.

- **Create invoices from a list of time and expenses.** If you have the Premier version you will see this option. Only choose it if you are going to be using the Invoice method of billing your clients versus the Statement Charge method. You may have to come back to this feature later when you decide which method you are going to use.

- **Mark all expenses as billable.** Selecting this option automatically marks your time as billable when you enter it. You can change it, but this is a great option to prevent you from forgetting to mark your billable time.

Figure 1.24 Company Preferences Tab

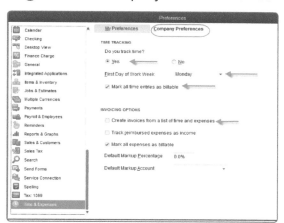

Take some time and go through the other options on the left. There are many different settings that you will notice when you go through each of the different categories, and while they may not make sense to you now, once you have been using the program for a bit, you will start to get a feel for changes that you would like to make.

I always suggest coming back to Preferences from time to time to see if there are any additional changes you would like to customize as you become more comfortable with the program. I have a detailed list of more options available at www.attorneytechnology.com/preferences.

Now that we have created our company data file, learned a little of the lingo, and set some preferences, it is time to talk about the Chart of Accounts.

Lesson 2

Chart of Accounts

Chart of accounts is an accounting term and is used as a way to organize the assets, liabilities, income, and expenses of a business. There are two main types of accounts: balance-sheet accounts and income-and-expense accounts.

- **Balance-Sheet Accounts** include all of your assets and liabilities. For example, your checking accounts are asset accounts. Your credit cards are your liability accounts.
- **Income-and-Expense Accounts** are different types of income, such as fee income and reimbursed expense income, and your expenses, such as advertising, office supplies, rent, and payroll.

Let's take a look at the default standard chart of accounts that comes with the company file we created. Because we chose Legal Services as our type of business, QuickBooks included a list of accounts for us to work with. This list is by no means complete, but it is a great starting point, and we can add, edit, or delete any of the accounts on the list.

From the Main Menu, choose *List* and *Chart of Accounts*. This standard list shows you the name and type of account and any balance that you may have in it.

The chart of accounts does not list a bank account, so we need to set that up now. We are going to create a bank account called Checking, which is the operating account from which you pay bills and into which you deposit money.

Click the **Account** button at the bottom of the window and choose **New** (see Figure 2.1).

Figure 2.1 Chart of Accounts: Adding a New Account

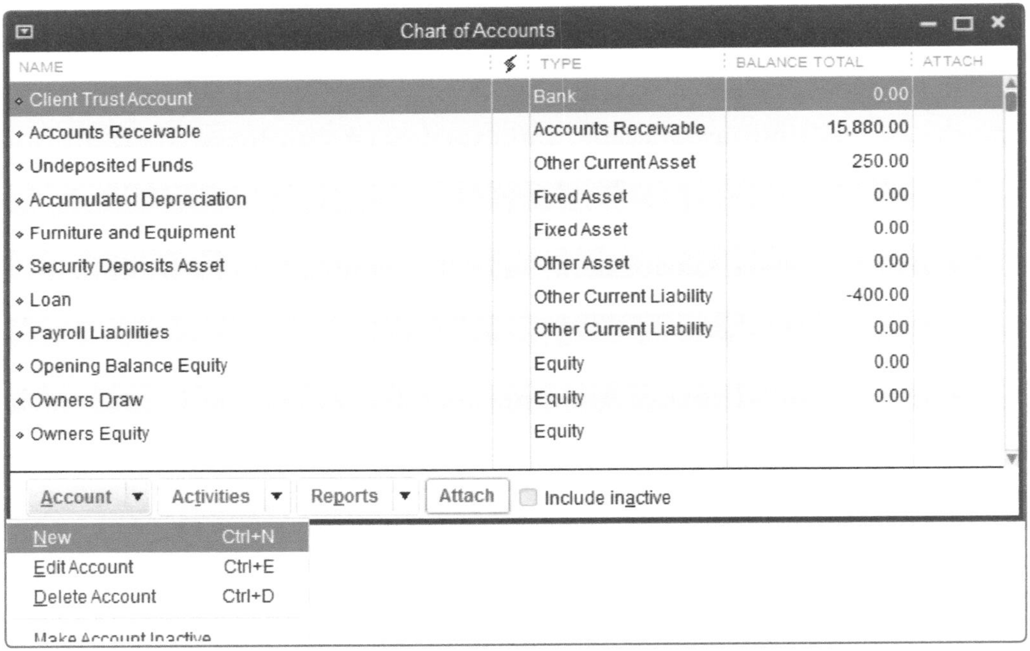

In the Add New Account: Choose Account Type window, choose **Bank** as the type and click **Continue** (see Figure 2.2).

Figure 2.2 Choosing the Account Type

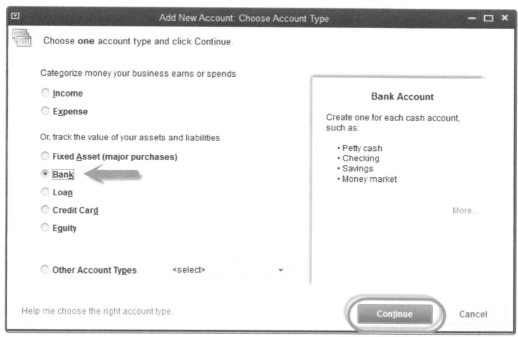

In the Add New Account window, you need to fill in some information (see Figure 2.3).

First is the account name and description. You can add other information if you like, but it is not required. Also, *do not enter an opening balance for the bank account* because QuickBooks will generate an entry to retained earnings. Instead, you probably

Figure 2.3 Add New Account

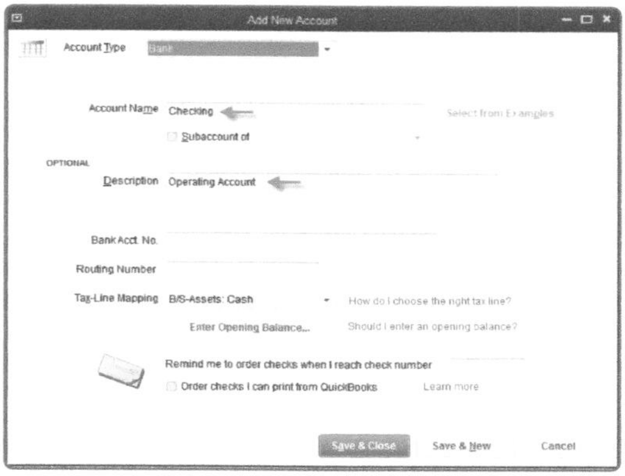

want to consult with your accountant and ask them to give you a balance sheet that you can use to enter the beginning entries into QuickBooks. I have a tutorial on my website showing you step by step how to enter beginning balances (www.attorneystechnology.com/BeginBalance). If you want to add other bank accounts, such as a savings account, click **Save & New**. If you are all finished, click **Save & Close**.

Now your bank account is part of the chart of accounts (see Figure 2.4). Take a moment to look over this list. You can edit or delete accounts that you don't think you need. Near the top of your list is a default account called Advanced Client Cost.

Figure 2.4
Chart of Accounts

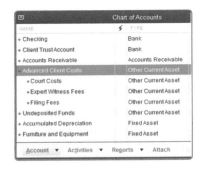

This is an account you can use for expenses paid from your operating account on behalf of a client. However, in certain tax situations, you cannot write client costs off until the case is settled. Every practice is different, so if you are not sure, this may be the time to call on your CPA or tax professional and ask how you should code expenses paid out of the operating account for client costs. Your tax professional may want you to code these expenses to another current asset or have you use an expense account.

As you use QuickBooks, you may find that you no longer need an account. For instance, let's say you opened a new bank account and closed the old one. You can make the old one inactive so you don't accidently deposit money into it. QuickBooks does not allow you to delete an account that has transactions associated with it, but making the account inactive hides it without deleting it. To make an account inactive, right click it and choose **Make Account Inactive** (see Figure 2.5).

As you look through the chart of accounts, you may also see expense categories that are missing. For example you might have a cleaning service for your office, and you want to track cleaning or janitorial expenses. You can add that expense account to your chart of accounts list.

Figure 2.5 Making an Account Inactive

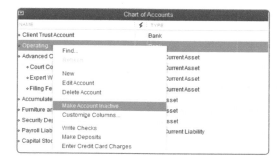

I recommend setting up an expense account for **Client Cost** and maybe one for **Research Fees**. I also recommend an income account called **Reimbursable Client Expense Income**, which will allow you to see the income that you received for costs. The Client Cost account will allow you to see what expenses you paid that are going to be reimbursed by the client.

To help you consider which accounts you might need, I have included a sample of a small law firm's chart of accounts in Appendix D.

For now, your chart of accounts is a work in progress. Throughout this book we will be adding accounts to the list, and you will be fine tuning it as you get more comfortable with QuickBooks.

Now that we have the chart of accounts set up, have our lingo down, and know how to move around in the program, it is time to start adding clients.

Customers & Jobs

Without clients in your law practice, you do not have much to do. QuickBooks is the same, so the first task is to get your clients set up.

Setting Up Your Clients

As we discussed in Lesson 1, QuickBooks uses the term **customers** for the list we will use to store your client information. You will add your clients' names and other relevant information to this list. How much information you include is up to you, and you can always add more information at a later time. To start, I recommend that you at least add the client's name, address, and a phone number (and e-mail address if you want to e-mail invoices or statements).

Let's get started adding some clients. Click the ***Customers*** icon from the top Icon Bar (or from the Main Menu choose ***Customers*** and then ***Customer Center***) to open up the Customer Center.

When the Customer Center opens, you will see a list of your clients on the left, and on the right you will see information about the client you have selected (see Figure 3.1). Until you add clients, the list is empty, so the next step is to add a few clients.

Figure 3.1 Adding Customer (Client) Information

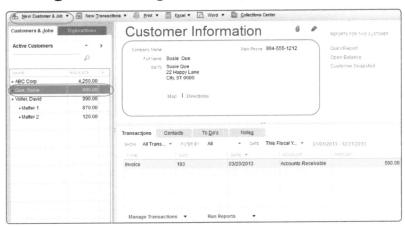

To add a new client, click the ***New Customer & Job*** button at the top left (see Figures 3.1 and 3.2).

The New Customer screen will appear, so you can add the basic information about a client (see Figure 3.3). Pay special attention to the **Invoice/Bill To** box. Whatever name and address you put in this box will show up on your invoices or statements.

Figure 3.2 New Customer & Jobs

Figure 3.3 New Customer Screen

Chose the ***Payment Settings*** tab on the left, so you can add your payment terms, the **Preferred Delivery Method** for invoices (for example, printing and mailing or e-mailing an invoice), and if you have the Premier edition only you may want to set the **Price Level** you are going to charge (see Figure 3.4). We will go over setting up and using Price Levels in Lesson 5. When you are finished, click *OK*.

You can also store the client's credit card information. However, if you are going to do this, you will want to enable QuickBooks Customer Credit Card Protection. When you enable this protection, you will be required to create a complex password for you and the other users of QuickBooks who can view this information. This password needs to be changed every ninety days.

Figure 3.4 Payment Settings

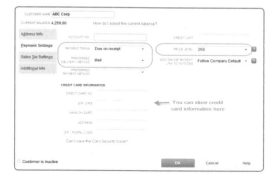

To enable the Customer Credit Card Protection, click *Company* from the Main Menu and Click *Customer Credit Card Protection*. You will see a dialog box like the one in Figure 3.5.

Take a few minutes and add a couple more clients to your client list. The next step is adding a Job to a client.

Figure 3.5 Enabling Customer Credit Card Protection

Setting Up Jobs for Clients

If you have a client for whom you handle different matters and you need to keep the information for each matter separate, you can do this by adding what QuickBooks calls a **Job**. For example, your client, ABC Corp., may have you handle several different litigation matters. To set this up in QuickBooks, you would create a customer called ABC Corp, and then you would add a Job called Matter 1, Jones vs ABC Corp, Case 123, or whatever name you use to keep track of different matters. Jobs keep each matter separate, while keeping all of one particular client's matters organized by that client. That way you can later generate individual reports by client or by client matter (job).

Remember, a Job is like a matter or case. It is used to keep billing information separate for each matter while grouping all of one client's matters together.

To set that up, click the client for whom you want to add a Job, and then click the ***New Customer & Job*** button at the top left. Select ***Add Job*** (see Figure 3.6).

Figure 3.7 shows the New Job window, which is pre-filled with the Customer information that you provided when you added the Customer. All you need to do is give the new case or matter a **Job Name** (see Figure 3.7). You can change the address and contact information for this job if you need to do so. Click ***OK*** when you're finished.

Figure 3.6
Add a Job for an
Existing Customer

Figure 3.7 Naming the Case or
Matter (Job Name)

Now when you look back at your Customer Center (see Figure 3.8) you can see the list of customers and Jobs in the left column. The Customer Center offers other great options: You can store multiple contacts related to a single case, create to-do lists, and add notes.

Click the **Contacts** tab and you will see a button at the bottom to **Manage Contacts** (see Figure 3.9a).

A window will appear that will allow you to add information about the contact (see Figure 3.9b).

Figure 3.8
Customer Center

Click **Save and Close** when you finish adding the information.

Figure 3.9a Adding Multiple Contacts for One Case

Figure 3.9b Enter Contact Information

Now let's look at the **To Do's** feature (see Figure 3.10). I love this feature because it is a great place to keep track of payment arrangements made with clients and tasks that need to be done.

Here you will see that you can choose the **Type** of To Do, set a **Priority** level, enter a **Due** date, and then enter **Details** to describe the task (see Figure 3.11).

Figure 3.10 To Do's

The Notes tab (shown in Figure 3.10 next to the To Do tab) is a feature I use all the time. When I am on a call with a client or in a training session with them, I enter a note with a brief description about what we discussed. This is helpful because when the client calls again, I can quickly go to the notes and see where we stopped. After clicking the *Notes* tab, click *Manage Notes* (see Figure 3.12).

Figure 3.11 Adding a To Do

Figure 3.12 Notes

You can **Date/Time Stamp** your note and add a description (see Figure 3.13). I really think you will like this feature. You could use it to track all the times a client says, "The check is in the mail."

Now is a good time to add a few more clients and Jobs. But remember that you do not need to add them all now. You will be coming back and adding new

Figure 3.13 Date/Time Stamp

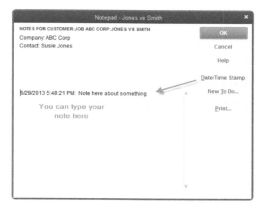

clients all the time as a part of your regular business. Get a handful added, and then let's move on to our next section, adding items.

Items & Services

To separate specific tasks or activities completed for a client, you may use billing codes. In QuickBooks, Items are the same as billing codes, and QuickBooks uses them to track time and create invoices or statement charges. You associate the Items you create with an income or an expense account from the Chart of Accounts.

We will work with two different types of Items in this lesson: service-type items and other-charge-type items.

The service-type item is used to track time that's billed to a client or create an invoice for a flat fee. For example, you can have service items that include:

- Legal fees
- Preparation of will
- Meeting with client
- Court appearance
- Research

The other-charge-type item is used when you bill your clients for costs. A few examples of cost items include:

- Postage
- Copies
- Mileage

But before we get too far, we need to stop and think about the income information you want to see. For example, do you want to know who billed what, or are you more interested in the type of service you provide, such as how much you billed for meetings, depositions, court appearances, or research? That answer determines how you want to set up your items.

For our example, we bill for time and we want to distinguish the income between two lawyers and the paralegal in the office. So we are going to set up our item list using their initials. This will enable us to create a report that will show how much each person billed and how much was received during a given period. Lesson 7 shows you how to track time and bill your clients and discusses integrating other time-and-billing software with QuickBooks.

Your office may want to track other things, so make sure that you spend a little time thinking about this now. To give you a little help, I have added examples of item lists in Appendix C.

Now that you have an idea of how you want to track your income, let's get started.

Adding Service Items

To get to the item list, go to the Home Page and click *Items & Services*. Your item list should come with a few preloaded items. Typically, Consulting and Postage and Delivery items are on the list, but we are going to add more. Click the *Item* button at the bottom and choose *New* (see Figure 4.1).

Figure 4.1 Adding an Item

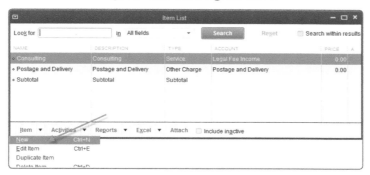

Figure 4.2 shows the New Item window where you can add detailed items such as a telephone conference, meeting with client, or draft letter. For our example, we want to be able to track income and billing by lawyer, so we will add a service-type item for one of our lawyers, Lynn Benton. Choose *Service* as the type and set up the first item for Lynn Benton by keying in her initials LB as the **Item Name/Number**. In the **Description** field we will type in Legal Fee and in the **Rate** field we will put in her standard billing rate of $250.00. For the **Account** field, we will choose an Income

Figure 4.2 The New Item Window

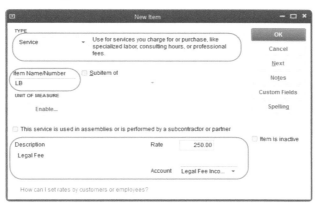

account. For this example choose ***Legal Fee Income***. If you were setting up an item specific to a type of service such as bankruptcy, you may wish to create an income account to track income related to these cases (Income accounts are described in Lesson 2).

When you've finished, click ***Next*** and you can enter another item.

Next we want to create an item to use for No Charge. You might be thinking, "An item for No Charge. Why?" There may be times that you want to show your client that you worked on matters for them, but you are not billing them for it. Or you may normally have things that you do for a client for no charge, and you want to keep track of those things. So let's create an item called LB-NC. This way we can use it to track the time and show the client this service without charging them for it. Another reason to set up this type of item is so you will be able to create a report by item to see how much time you have spent on no-charge work.

Figure 4.3 shows how to enter information: In the **Item Name/Number** box, enter LB-NC, and in the **Description**, add something like No Charge, and give it a rate of $0. For the **Account**, select ***Legal Fee Income***. Click the ***Next*** button to add another item.

Figure 4.3 Creating a New Item

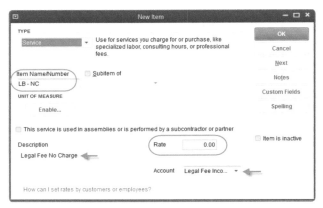

You also need an item to track write-offs because while preparing client bills, you may decide to write off some of the time you spent on the work. This item will allow you to do that, and track it so that you can generate a report in the future to see how much time you have written off. Remember, if you have multiple lawyers working in the office, add a write-off item for each lawyer. Again, this will enable you to create a report for any given period on how much each lawyer wrote off and for which clients.

Enter the Item Name/Number, something like LB-Write Off; Enter the Description as Write Off; set the Rate to 0.00, and choose *Legal Fee Income* as the Account (see Figure 4.4), or create another income account called Write-Offs.

Figure 4.4 Creating a Write-Off Item

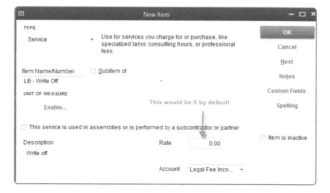

Take a few minutes and add the same items in for the other lawyer and the paralegal, and when you are finished, your item list will be ready to start tracking time that you can bill to your clients (see Figure 4.5).

Figure 4.5 Service Items

Adding Cost Items

Now we need to set up items to track costs that you pay out of your operating account and for which you want to bill your clients (see Figure 4.6). These are *only* used for the operating account and *not anything related to the Trust or Escrow account.*

On the item list, click **New** to add a cost item (see Figure 4.1). Choose **Other Charge** as the type, and select the option **This item is used in assemblies or is a reimbursable charge**. For the **Expense Account**, choose **Client Cost,** and for the **Income Account**, choose **Reimbursable Client Expense Income**.

There is no need to add a cost or a sales price at this point, as these items may vary in costs depending on the client and the matter. We can add the cost when we use the item.

Figure 4.6 Creating a Cost That Can Be Billed to a Client

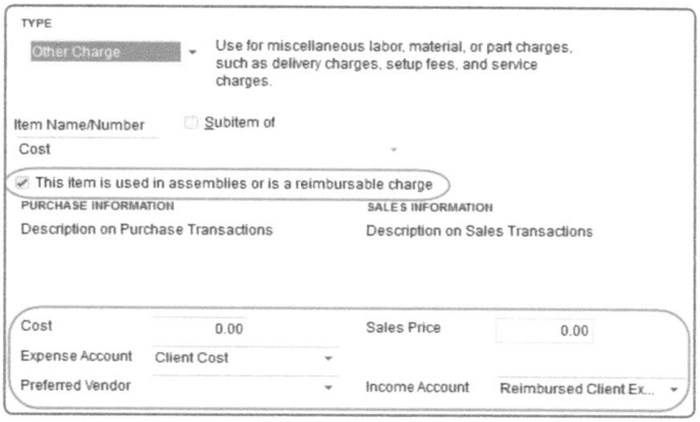

If you want to take some time now to add more items, feel free to do so. We are going to use these items in Lesson 7, Time Tracking.

Price Levels

The **Price Levels** feature is only available in QuickBooks Premier Edition, and is one of its most popular features. It is an option that allows you to set a rate you bill a particular client. For example, your normal billing rate might be $250 an hour but you have a client you only want to bill at $225. You can create a price level for the $225 an hour and assign the rate to that client. As you track your time for that client, QuickBooks uses the correct billing rate. But Price Levels offers other useful options. For example, you may find that some lengthy client matters extend over a period during which you raised your rates. Price Levels lets you retain the earlier agreed-upon rate with those older clients while your new clients get the new rate.

> **NOTE:** Price levels are part of QuickBooks Premier but not QuickBooks Pro. While you can work around this limitation in QuickBooks Pro, if you frequently bill different rates for different clients, make it much easier on yourself and get QuickBooks Premier.

First, we need to make sure you have the preference set to use Price Levels. From the Main Menu, click *Edit* and then click *Preferences*. On the left side, go to *Sales & Customers* and click the *Company Preferences* tab to check that the option for Price Levels is checked (see Figure 1.17).

Next, we need to set up the Price Levels. From the Main Menu, click **List** and select **Price Levels**.

Click **Price Level** at the bottom of the window and then click **New** (see Figure 5.1).

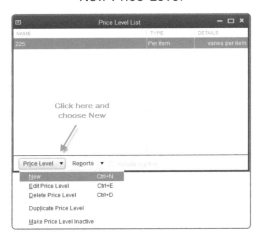

Figure 5.1 Creating a New Price Level

- In the **Price Level Name** box, enter a name for this price level (see Figure 5.2). For this example, we are setting up a price level of $225 per hour, so a logical name for this level is 225.
- For Price Level, select the option **Per Item**.
- Click the **Adjust** button
- Select the items that you want to change the rate for and enter the amount in the **Custom Price** column.
- Click **OK** when done.

Figure 5.2 Editing the Price Level

All the clients that we assign with this price level will get a rate of $225. This will simplify tracking your time and billing your clients because QuickBooks chooses the correct billing rate for your client. The key is to make sure that you assign this price level to the client.

Setting Up Client Price Level

Now we want to edit a client to use this price level. Go to your **Customers List** and select a client that you want to add a price level to. Click the **Edit** icon for that customer (see Figure 5.3).

Figure 5.3 Changing a Client Price Level

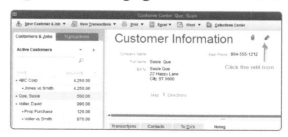

If you are using Quick-Books 2012 or earlier versions, click the **Additional Info** tab. For QuickBooks 2013, click **Payment Settings** (see Figure 5.4).

Figure 5.4 Payment Settings

Next, choose the price level in the **Price Level** box.

Click **OK** when done.

Now every time you bill this client on this job—Susie Que in this example—this price level will show as $225 per hour for billing.

Let's take a second to reflect on the last few sections. We have learned to add customers, add separate jobs for separate matters for a particular customer, and we have set up our billable items. We have set up price levels and assigned the price levels for those clients.

Now you might think that it is time to enter time so that we can create a bill, but not so fast. Before we can do that we need to set up our employees in QuickBooks so we can track time, and we start that by looking at the Payroll module.

Payroll

QuickBooks allows you to process payroll for your employees, as well as process required quarterly and annual federal tax returns. This service is considered an add-on to QuickBooks and you must pay extra for the service and activate it before you can prepare payroll checks.

You may or may not want to use the QuickBooks Payroll module. You may already have a service that takes care of this for you, or you may not have employees. If that is the case, feel free to skip the payroll setup section and jump to the adding employees section. I would, however, encourage you to look into the service if you are paying a third party to handle it for you. Even QuickBooks' basic service Payroll Module can save you money—and even time—if you let QuickBooks handle it instead of a third party.

Turning On Payroll

QuickBooks currently has three payroll services available: Basic, Enhanced, and Full Service (see Figure 6.1). The Basic edition allows you to prepare paychecks and your accountant to process the payroll tax returns. The Enhanced allows you to prepare paychecks and generate the forms for the payroll returns. The Full Service allows you to do paychecks and leave the rest to QuickBooks.

By default the payroll feature is turned on. If it is turned off, you can turn it on by clicking on **Edit** and then **Preferences.** Then click **Payroll & Employees** in the left panel (see Figure 6.2). Next, click the Company Preferences tab and choose **Full Payroll**.

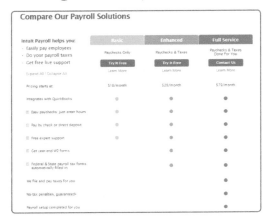

Figure 6.1 Payroll Options

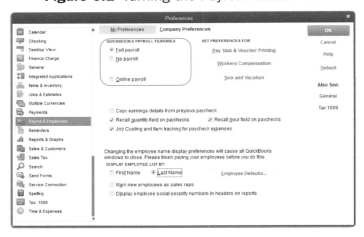

Figure 6.2 Turning the Payroll Feature On

Now that payroll is turned on, you are ready to choose your service. From the Home Page, click the **Turn on Payroll** icon (see Figure 6.3), and QuickBooks will guide you through choosing the service you prefer.

Figure 6.3 Choosing a Payroll Service

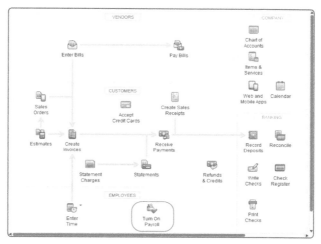

Payroll Items

Payroll items are used to track individual amounts on a paycheck and tally the accumulated year-to-date wage and tax amounts for each employee.

The **Payroll Item List** comes pre-loaded with some common items such as Hourly Wages, Federal Tax Withholding, and Social Security Tax. You may find that you need to add a payroll item such as Holiday Pay. To get to the Payroll Item List shown in Figure 6.4, click *List* from the Main Menu and choose *Payroll Item List*. (You must have payroll turned on to see this choice.)

Figure 6.4 Payroll Item List

ITEM NAME	TYPE	AM...	LIMIT	ANN...	TAX TRACK...	PA
Hourly Wages	Hourly Wage				Compensat...	
Overtime	Hourly Wage				Compensat...	
Advance Earned I...	Federal Tax				Advance EI...	
Federal Unemplo...	Federal Tax	0.6%	7,00...	7,00...	FUTA	
Federal Withholdi...	Federal Tax				Federal	
Medicare Company	Federal Tax	1.45%			Comp. Med...	
Medicare Employ...	Federal Tax	1.45%			Medicare	
Social Security C...	Federal Tax	6.2%	113,7...	113,7...	Comp. SS ...	
Social Security E...	Federal Tax	6.2%	-113...	-113...	SS Tax	

Payroll Item ▼	Activities ▼	Reports ▼	
New	Ctrl+N		
Edit Payroll Item	Ctrl+E		
Delete Payroll Item	Ctrl+D		

To add a new payroll item, click the **Payroll Item** button at the bottom and choose **New**.

Leave **EZ Setup** selected (see Figure 6.5) unless you are an *expert* user and click **Next**.

QuickBooks displays the Add New Payroll Item window, which takes you through the steps of the payroll item set up process (see Figure 6.6). Select the type of payroll item you want to create, and then click **Next**.

QuickBooks will then open the Payroll Setup Window. Follow the on-screen instructions to create the payroll item. When you are finished, click **Finish**. Close the Payroll Item list.

Figure 6.5 Payroll Setup Method

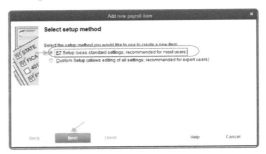

Figure 6.6 Add New Payroll Item

Adding Employees

Payroll is all set up, and you are now ready to add employees. Click **Employees** from the Home Page or from the Main Menu to open the **Employee Center**.

The Employee Center is similar to the Customer Center. Your employees' names are listed on the left, and the information you enter about the selected employee is displayed on the right. To add an employee, click the **New Employee** button at the top (see Figure 6.7).

Figure 6.7 Employee Center

Select the **_Personal_** tab in the New Employee window, and you can add the first name, middle initial, last name, Social Security number, gender, and date of birth (see Figure 6.8).

Figure 6.8 Entering Personal Information

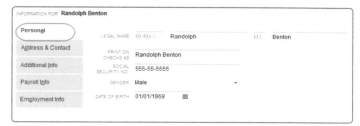

Choose the **_Address & Contact_** tab to enter the employee's contact information (see Figure 6.9).

Figure 6.9 Address & Contact Tab

The **Additional Info** tab in Figure 6.10 has a section for adding custom fields, such as emergency contact information or a spouse's name, for each employee.

Figure 6.10 Additional Info

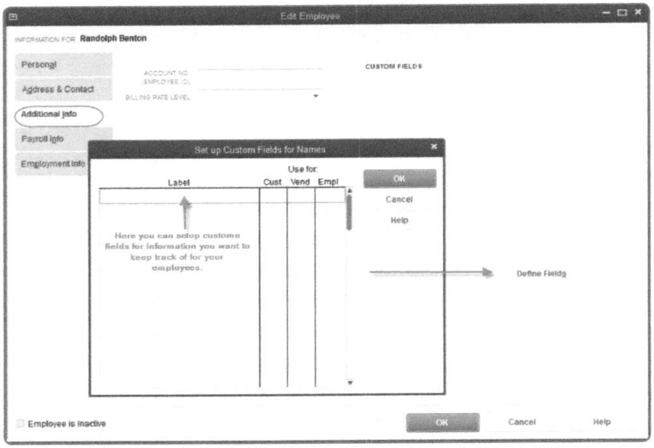

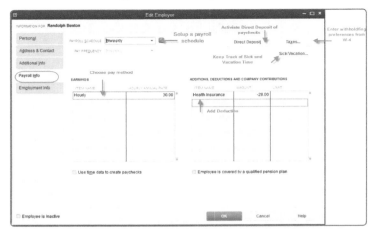

In the **Payroll Info** tab, you can set up and choose Payroll Schedules, Pay Frequency, Direct Deposit, and Taxes and keep track of sick and vacation time (see Figure 6.11).

Figure 6.11 Payroll Info

In the **Employment Info** Tab, you can keep track of hire and release dates (see Figure 6.12).

If you are not going to be doing payroll in QuickBooks, you don't need to fill in all the other information; an employee name is what's needed for employees to have the ability to enter their time. When you are finished, click **OK**.

Figure 6.12 Employment Info Tab

Time Tracking

With QuickBooks you don't need to have a separate legal time-and-billing software package because you can enter time and create the invoice within QuickBooks.

Although QuickBooks can do it all, if you have practice management software such as MyCase, Clio, Tabs, Timeslips, or Amicus, it probably has a time feature in it. Most of the other software that I have seen lawyers use has a module or a link that can send the data to QuickBooks.

Some programs send the time data as time sheets and some send billing data as invoices. I recommend researching whether your practice management software links to QuickBooks and how it integrates before you initiate any link from it to QuickBooks. For some programs the integration is simple, while others might require a call to your practice management software company's customer support to get it up and running.

> **NOTE:** Before you do anything that integrates with QuickBooks or changes QuickBooks in any way, make sure that you always make a backup copy of your QuickBooks data before doing anything, including linking your practice management software. We cover backing up in the last section: Final Notes.

We have set up our clients, items, and timekeepers (certain employees) in QuickBooks. Now we want to be able to enter the time that we spend on our cases so that we can generate a bill. But, before you can create that bill for time worked, you need to enter time in a timesheet.

Time Tracking

QuickBooks has two basic ways you can enter time manually: the Weekly Timesheet and the Single Activity. The Weekly Timesheet allows you to enter in time like a spreadsheet—entering different activities in a one-week view—while with the Single Activity window, you enter one item at a time per client. Both have their merits, so we will take a look at each.

Single Activity

From the Home Page, choose ***Enter Time***, and you will see options for **Use Weekly Timesheet** and **Time/Enter Single Activity** (see Figure 7.1). We will start with the Time/Enter Single Activity.

When you choose Time/Enter Single Activity, a window will appear as shown in Figure 7.2.

Figure 7.1 Options for Entering Time

Figure 7.2 Time/Enter Single Activity

First, enter the *Date* of the activity. Next, in the *Name* field choose the timekeeper, select the *Customer* or *Customer Job* (if you are using jobs), and select the *Service Item* (discussed in Lesson 4) for this activity. In the *Duration* box, enter the total amount of time spent on the activity. Or you can let QuickBooks track the time for you.

In the Notes box, you can add a description of what you did, but be careful. What you key in here will show up on your client's invoices. You have plenty of room to be as detailed as you like.

A **Billable** check box is in the upper right corner of the window. Check this box if you want this activity to show up on the invoice. If the time entry is not billable, un-check the checkmark and continue tracking your time. For example, you would uncheck the box to track administrative functions or time off.

In the bottom left corner is a little timer that you can use to track time when you are working on a task (see Figure 7.3). Just open the window, fill in the appropriate information and click *Start*. The timer will begin tracking time. When you are finished, click *Stop* (or Pause) and enter your notes. You can adjust the time if you want to round it up or down.

Figure 7.3 Timer

The weekly timesheet does not have an option to use the timer. If you like this feature, you will need to use the Enter Single Activity option. Activities tracked using the single activity option will populate the Weekly Timesheet so you can see all of the activities in one place.

Weekly Timesheet

The Weekly Timesheet option is an easy-to-use grid in which you can enter your time directly, or view all the time you have entered in the single activity window. Click *Enter Time* from the Home Page and choose *Weekly Timesheet*.

Figure 7.4 Weekly Timesheet

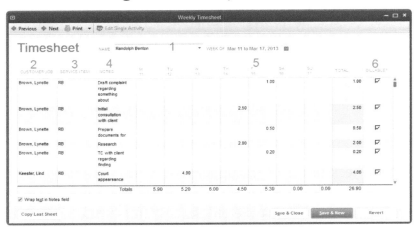

As shown in Figure 7.4, the Weekly Timesheet is a grid-like spreadsheet where you can enter or modify your time information. Personally, I like this method of entering my time the best because I can see totals for the day at the bottom. When the afternoon rolls around, I had better see some billable hours on my timesheet. If you use the Enter Single Activity option for entering time, all of your entries will show in the Weekly Timesheet grid.

We are going to look at the different parts of the screen—the numbers below correspond to the numbers in Figure 7.4.

1. **Name.** This is the timekeeper's (employee's) name. Choose your own name from the list.

2. **Customer Job.** Here you will choose the client name or client job that you are entering time for.

3. **Service Item.** This is the service that you are going to be using for billing.

4. **Notes.** Enter a description about what you did. Remember that this description will appear on the invoice or statement for the client.

5. **Days of the Week.** Pick the day of the week that you worked on the activity and enter the amount of time spent.

6. **Billable?** If you want the entry to show up on an invoice or statement, select the billable box.

I suggest that you try each of the options before deciding which method works best for you. It might take some practice entering time before you get a feel for what is most comfortable. And remember there is no right or wrong way to do it.

Now that we have some time in, let's go to the next step—generating time reports.

Reporting on Time

The next step is to generate reports on the time activities. These reports will give us a chance to review billable time and identify which clients to invoice.

To get time reports, go to the Main Menu and click **Reports**. Then choose **Report Center** (see Figure 8.1).

The resulting window (see Figure 8.2) has a list of categories or types of reports on the left. Choose one, and it will display the reports available on the right. Choose **Jobs, Time & Mileage** on the left and select **Time by Job Summary** on the right. Then click **Run** to see the report.

Figure 8.1
Accessing the
Report Center

Figure 8.2 Selecting a Report

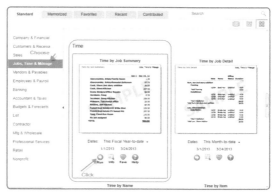

When the report is displayed on the screen, you will see the client's name, service item used for tracking time, and the amount of time charged to the client (see Figure 8.3).

Figure 8.3 Time by Job Summary Report

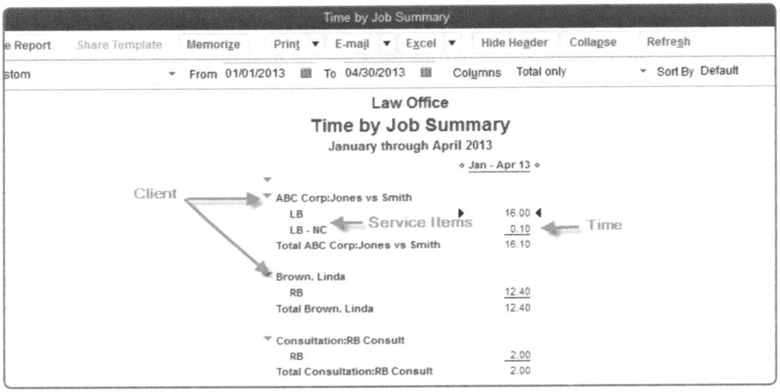

As with many of the preloaded reports that come with QuickBooks, you may want to customize this report. We can change any number of options by showing and hiding parts of the report. For example, if you wanted to see a report showing only the clients you worked on and the amount of time you spend on each one, you would customize the report to only show one timekeeper (you) and % of billable time spent. For example, you could create a report showing how much time was spent in depositions (by everyone in the firm and also by the timekeeper), how much time was spent answering interrogatories (by everyone in the firm and also by the timekeeper), and how much time was spent writing summary judgments (by everyone in the firm and also by the timekeeper).

Click the ***Customize Report*** button at the top left side of the report (see Figure 8.4).

Figure 8.4 Customizing a Report

Choose the ***Display*** tab, and check ***Billed***, ***Unbilled***, and ***% of Column***. This will give us all billed and unbilled time and show us percentage of time spent on each client. To see how much time you are not billing, check ***Not Billable*** (see Figure 8.5).

Figure 8.5 Choosing Report Criteria

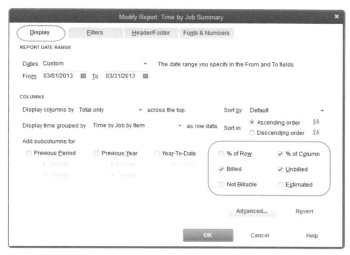

Now click the ***Filters*** tab at the top of the window. Here is where you can select a single employee to view. In the Filter box, click ***Name***, and then select the employee from the drop-down menu whose time you want to view (see Figure 8.6). You will notice that the filter is added to the current Filter choices on the right.

Figure 8.6 Adding Report Filters

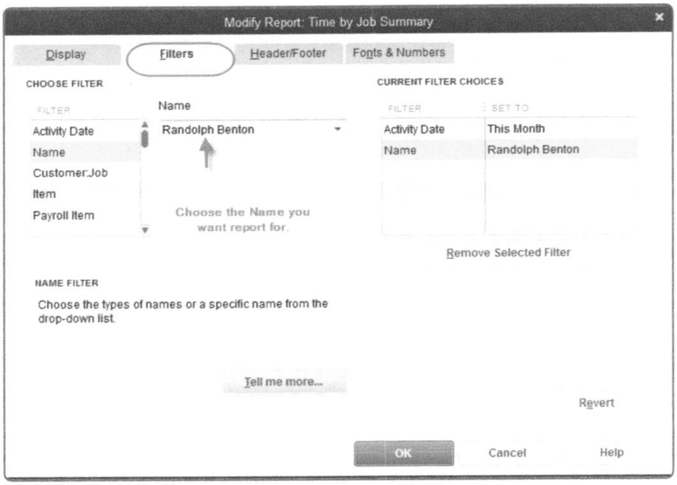

One last step—we are going to modify the title of the report so that we can identify the modifications that we have made. Click the ***Header/Footer*** tab at the top of the window (see Figure 8.7). In the Report Title box, we are going to change the title to RB—Billed and Billable Time Summary to reflect that this is a summary of the time for the employee RB.

Figure 8.7 Customizing the Report Name

Click *OK* to view the new customized report.

Figure 8.8 Customized Report

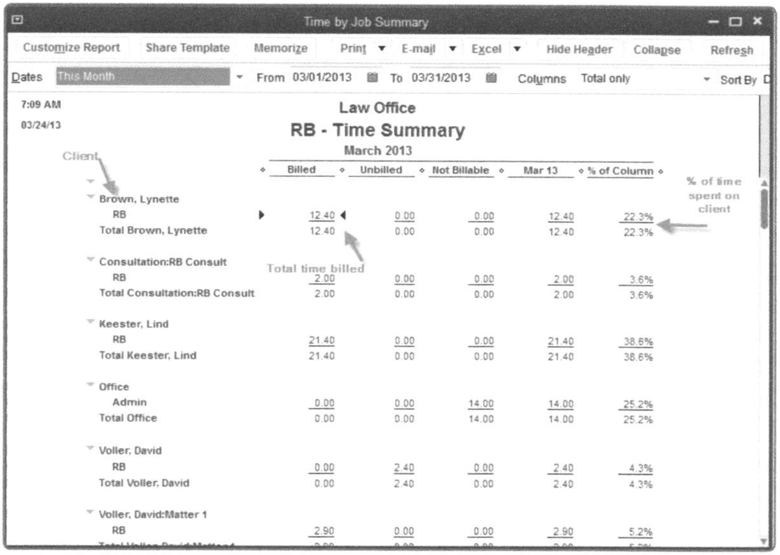

Figure 8.8 shows RB's time for the month of March. Each client is listed in the left column and the amount of time spent on each client is listed across the row. The last column shows the percentage of time spent on that client.

Another great report for reviewing your time before you do billing is the **Time by Job Detail**. This report allows you to view the individual time entries for each client along with the *first 99 characters* of the actual notes.

> **NOTE:** Although this report only displays the first 99 characters of the Notes field, the entire note appears on the invoice or statement.

Now we will create a report that shows the detail of time spent on each client so we can determine which clients to invoice.

Click the **Reports Center**, choose **Time, Jobs & Mileage** (see Figures 8.1 and 8.2), and click the **Time by Job Detail** Report (see the right side of Figure 8.2). By default the report only shows client name, timekeeper, and duration. To see the description of work, click the **Customize** button when the report is displayed. Then go to the **Display** tab and choose **Notes** (see Figure 8.9).

Figure 8.9 Customizing Time by Job Detail Reports

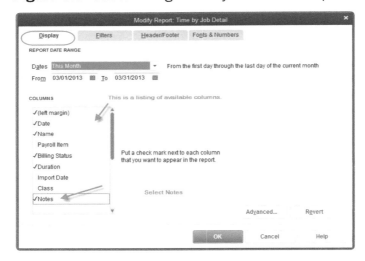

Click **OK** to view the report. Now you can see the client and all the timekeepers who did billable work for that client, and you can also see the notes (see Figure 8.10).

Figure 8.10 Customized Time by Job Detail Report

Once you have customized a report that you will want to use regularly, you can memorize it so you don't have to customize each time. I will show you in the next lesson how to memorize reports and create groups. For now, simply click the ***Memorize*** button at the top of the report and give it a name (see Figure 8.11).

Figure 8.11 Memorize Button

Next time you want to generate that report it will be customized already. Go to the Main Menu and click **Reports**, **Memorized Reports**, choose **Memorize Report List** (see Figure 8.12). There's no need to go through the process of customizing, because this report is already customized.

Figure 8.12
Memorized Reports

Memorizing reports can be a huge time saver, especially when you create reports that you want to generate on a routine basis. But we are going to take it a step further in the next lesson and show you the power of the Memorized Report Groups.

Memorizing Reports

As you learned in the last lesson, QuickBooks reports have a good deal of flexibility. Being able to customize reports allows you to massage the data to get exactly what you need. You may find that you use some reports frequently. The ability to memorize a report helps insure that the time that you spend getting a report to look just right and contain just the right information is not wasted. Some examples of reports you might want to memorize include Unbilled Time, Unbilled Cost, Billing by Timekeeper and Income by Timekeeper.

QuickBooks even takes it a step further and allows you to organize your memorized reports into groups so you can easily find and generate them. For example, at billing time you will probably have a few customized reports (e.g., Unbilled Time, Unbilled Cost, and Billing by Timekeeper) that you want to run each time. QuickBooks allows you to create a report group. We will call ours **-Billing Reports**. You can put all your custom memorized reports in that group, making it very easy to find and generate them when the time comes. And no, the dash in front is not a typo—I will explain why as you read on.

First we are going to create a report group and then add a few reports to show you how to do it.

First, click **Reports > Memorized Reports**, and choose **Memorized Reports List** (see Figure 9.1).

Figure 9.1 Creating a Group of Memorized Reports

You will see a listing of all your memorized reports (see Figure 9.2). Click the **Memorized Report** button at the bottom and choose **New Group**.

Figure 9.2 List of Memorized Reports

We are going to create a group called -Billing Reports. Click **OK** and your group will be created. Now when you look at the list of Memorized reports, you will see your new group right there at the top.

Now for a little trick. The reason I put the hyphen in front of the report title is so the report shows up at the top of the list and I know it is a report I created, not one of the preloaded memorized reports from QuickBooks. From now on, when I customize a report I plan on using during billing time, I can save it in that group and it will show up at the top of the list.

Now that we have our new group, let's add a few reports to it. Go to the Main Menu and click **Reports**, **Memorized Reports** and then **Memorized Report List**. In this list, find the report that you created in the last lesson, **RB—Time Detail** and click it. Then click the **Memorized Report** button at the bottom, and this time select **Edit Memorized Report** (see Figure 9.3).

Figure 9.3 Editing a Memorized Report

Here you will see the option to *Save in Memorized Report Group*. Check that option, and then choose the group on the right to add it to, the new -Billing Reports group.

You will see this option each time you memorize a new report, so just remember to check the box and add the report when you first memorize it, so you can save yourself a few steps.

Now that we have generated and memorized a few reports—by creating a custom report group and adding all of our reports—our billing just got easier. You can now select to print multiple reports, or even all the reports in the group at one time. Here's how.

Click *Reports*, *Memorized Reports*, and then *Memorized Report List*. Next, select *-Billing Reports*, and click the *Display* button at the bottom. The Process Multiple Reports window will show. By default all the reports are checked, but you can click to remove the check in front of any reports you don't want to print this time. Choose whether you want to *Display* or *Print* them by selecting the button at the bottom (see Figure 9.4).

Figure 9.4 Viewing the Reports

Now all of the reports that you selected will display or print in one click. This will save a good deal of time when billing time rolls around.

So far: we have added our clients, set up our service and cost times, and added our employees. We have also added in some time and created a few reports so we can review our time in preparation for billing clients. Now we are ready to get started billing.

Billing Clients

Now that we have our time added it is time to start billing our clients. Before we get started though, we need to choose our billing method, and set up our invoice or statement.

Choosing a Method

QuickBooks offers two ways to bill clients: the Statement Charge Method and the Invoice Method. Which one do you want to use? Here are the big differences.

- The **Invoice Method** works great if you do billing once a month or if you bill a flat rate for services like Wills & Trust, Consultations, or Bankruptcy.
- The **Statement Charge Method** is a way to bill for each activity separately. It allows you to create a detailed statement for any time period, and it will show the detail of each charge.

If you work on cases on which you need to be able to provide a detailed statement over a long period of time, you may want to consider the Statement Charge Method. It allows you to bill your clients monthly, show the beginning balance, payments received, and ending balance. The downside to this method is that you really are limited to the customization, in that you cannot group or order the transactions on the statement; it is all date driven. It is the best method to choose if you need the ability to create detailed reports of your activity or costs charged to the client.

Many lawyers prefer creating invoices and attaching a statement to it if the client has a prior balance due. If you have the Premier edition of QuickBooks you can create invoices for your time and expenses for all clients in one screen. If you do an extensive amount of billing each month, this may be a better choice. If you do a lot of flat rate work, the Invoice Method is almost certainly a better option. I also like this method because it allows more customization to the printed invoice.

My website (www.AttorneysTechnology.com/templates) has samples of and templates for each method that you can download. It also offers some other cool tricks on how to group transactions (see www.attorneys technology.com/creating-an-invoice-in-quickbooks-grouped-by-timekeeper).

For the example here, we are going to choose the Invoice Method. We have already entered our time but before we start generating our invoices, we are going to customize the invoice to look a little better than the ones that come preloaded with QuickBooks.

Customizing the Invoice

QuickBooks is installed with a few different invoice templates. Two of them, **Attorney's Invoice** and **Time & Expense Invoice**. They, are really close to what we want, but they do not include a column for date of service. Once again, QuickBooks has the flexibility to customize these templates and save them so we can easily use them.

To customize a template, go to the Main Menu and choose *List* and then *Templates*. This will display a list of all the templates available in QuickBooks. We are going to make a copy of the Attorney's Invoice, customize it, and then give it a custom name. By copying the invoice first, we are keeping the original so it will also be there in case we need it later.

To duplicate the invoice, click the *Templates* button at the bottom, then select *Duplicate* (see Figure 10.1).

Figure 10.1 Duplicating the Template

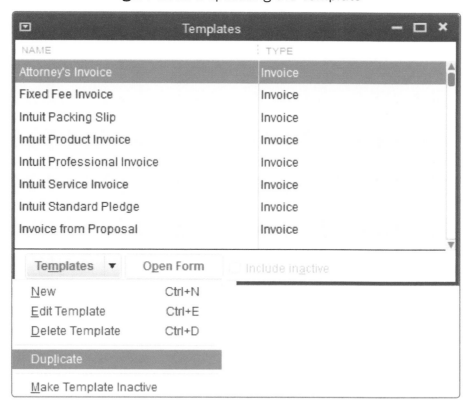

You will be prompted to select the type of template you are creating, and you should select ***Invoice***. Then click ***OK***. You will see your new invoice in the Templates box with the name Copy of Attorney's Invoice.

Now we are going to edit the template to customize it. Click ***Copy of Attorney's Invoice***. Then click the ***Templates*** button at the bottom and choose ***Edit Template***.

Now you will see the Basic Customization window, which displays a thumbnail image of what your template will look like on the right (see Figure 10.2).

Figure 10.2 Basic Customization Window

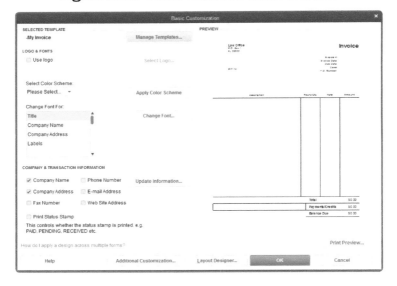

There are a few things that you can do in this window to customize the invoice. First, if you have a logo and want to display it, you can insert it by clicking the box for ***Use logo***. A window will appear to allow you to navigate to your logo. Click ***Open*** once you find the efile of your logo (see Figure 10.3).

Figure 10.3 Customizing with a Logo

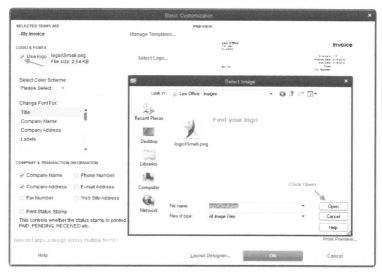

Now the logo appears on the invoice (see Figure 10.4).

Figure 10.4 Copy of Attorney's Invoice Customized with Logo

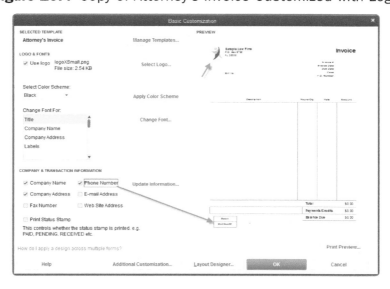

You can also include your phone number on the invoice as shown in Figure 10.4. Now we want to change the headers and add a new column for the date, so we are going to go a little further. As shown in Figure 10.5, click the ***Additional Customization*** button at the bottom of the window to bring up additional ways to customize the invoice.

Figure 10.5 The Additional Customization Button

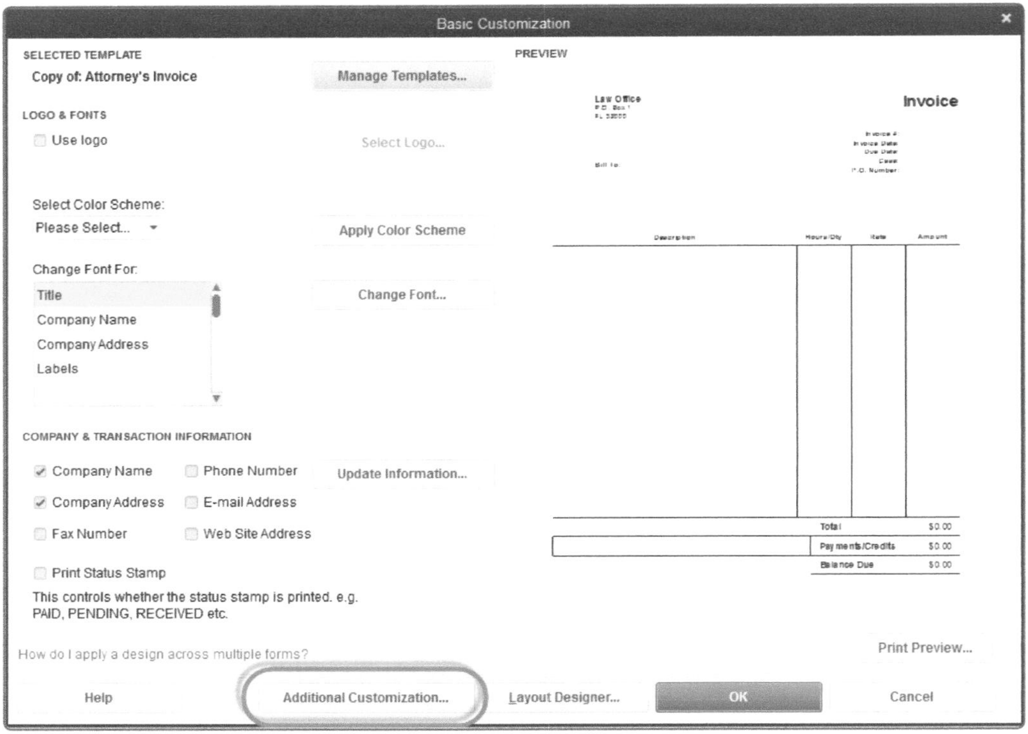

When the window appears you will notice the first tab is the Header tab (see Figure 10.6). The header is the top portion of your invoice, and this option allows you to rename, reorder, remove, and add columns.

Figure 10.6 Additional Customization Options

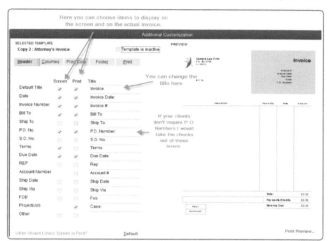

On the left are several tabs for the different sections of the template. Since we want to add a column, click the ***Columns*** tab and you will see a window like Figure 10.7.

Figure 10.7 Customizing Invoice Columns

Here you have options for the columns you want to use in the invoice.

Because you may want the service date on the invoice, find the Service Date column and add a check in both the *Screen* and *Print* boxes. The Screen box will allow you to hide or view the column when you are viewing and creating the invoice. The Print box will hide or show the column when you print. So it is possible to show the column when viewing on the screen, and then hide it when you print it. Generally you would want to show the service date, but there is other information you may not want clients to see. For example, you may want to see the rate but don't want the rate to print on the invoice.

You can choose what order you want the columns in by entering a number into the blank box in the column labeled **Order** at the right. Here we entered **1** in the Service Date column, so the service date will be the first column on the invoice. You can change the name of a column (e.g., we changed Service Date to Date by entering the word Date into the **Title** box). The right side of the screen shows a preview of what the invoice will look like.

When you have finished, click *OK* to save your changes. Take a few minutes to look at the other options, and make any additional changes that you want now. Remember, you can come back at any time and adjust any of these options, and it may take a few times to get it just right.

Now click the *Layout Designer* button at the bottom of the window in Figure 10.7. A new window will appear like the one in Figure 10.8. Here you can move things around, change fonts, and add colors. Downloadable templates with instructions on importing them into your QuickBooks are available at my website just for you (see www.AttorneysTechnology.com/abaTemplates).

Figure 10.8 Designing the Layout

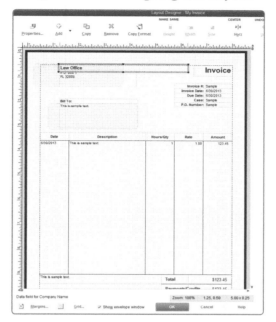

When you are ready, click **OK** at the bottom to get back to the Basic Customization screen.

We are almost finished, but we want to change the name of the template so we can find it easily. To do this, click the ***Manage Templates*** button shown in Figure 10.9 to open the Manage Templates window. Click ***Copy of Attorney's Invoice*** (the invoice we just customized) in the list on the left. Find the Template Name box on the right and enter whatever name you'd like for this customized invoice. For our example, I am going to use—**My Invoice**.

Figure 10.9 Naming the Customized Invoice

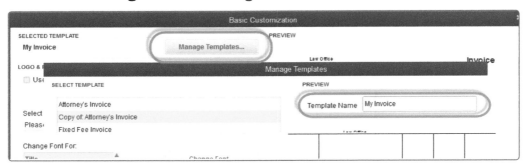

Once again, here is the little trick to make the invoice appear at the top of the list. That's right, add that hyphen in front of the name so it will always be easy to find.

Click **OK** once to close the Manage Templates window, and then click **OK** again to close the Basic Customization window.

Getting the invoices to look just right might take a little going back and forth. Take your time and make them like you want them. Then when you are ready, we can start generating invoices.

Billing Process

Now it is billing time, and here is a quick checklist of the things that we need to do to get started. Don't get overwhelmed. Honestly, once you get the hang of it you will find it is easy.

- Make sure all time is entered.
- Print or display the Unbilled Time Report and Unbilled Cost Report.
- Create invoices.
- Add any additional costs to the invoices.
- Print or e-mail the invoices. *If you have a trust or escrow account you may want to transfer the funds and apply the transfers to the invoices before you print out the invoices.*

- Run any billing reports you want.
- Take a coffee break because you are done.

Report on Unbilled Time

Once your time is entered, the first thing you should do is run a report that shows you all your unbilled time. This way you have a list of everyone that needs to be invoiced.

From the Main Menu, click **Reports** and choose **Jobs, Time &** **Mileage**. Locate the **Time by Jobs Detail** report and click it to open it. Click the **Customize** button on the top left, and then click the **Filters** tab. In the Filter box, scroll down to find **Billing Status** and click it. To the right, click in the **Unbilled** option (see Figure 10.10).

Figure 10.10 Report Unbilled Time

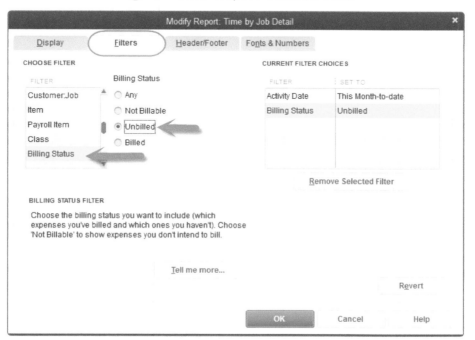

Next click the ***Header/Footer*** tab and enter a report title such as Unbilled Time by Job Detail (see Figure 10.11).

Figure 10.11 Naming the Unbilled Time Report

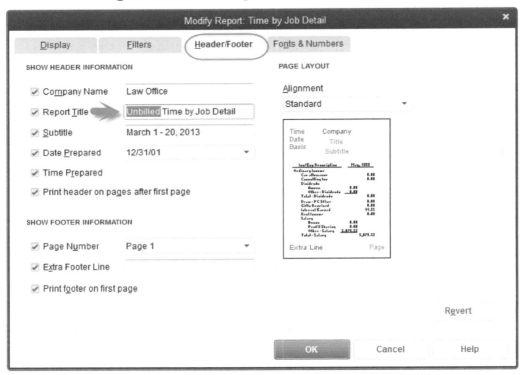

Make any other modifications that you want, and then click **OK**.

The report in Figure 10.12 shows you all the time you have entered that has not been billed to a client. You can change the date range to show whatever period you would like. I find it useful to set the date to **All** so that each time it comes up you don't have to change the dates. Another good reason for setting it to All is to be sure you didn't leave out any billing from a prior period.

Now that you have your Unbilled Time by Job Detail report let's memorize it so you don't have to customize each month. Click the ***Memorize*** button at the top of the window.

Figure 10.12 Unbilled Time by Job Detail

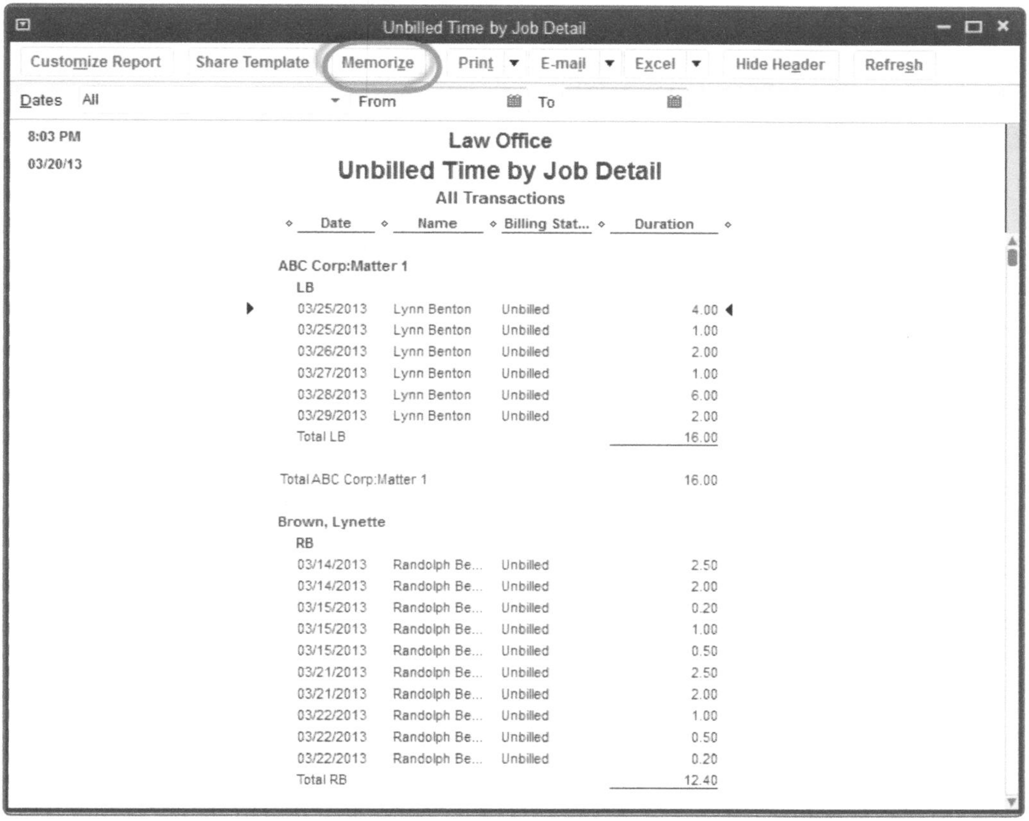

You may want to print the report at this point, or just keep it open on the screen so that you can refer to it. We are going to use this report as a reference to generate our invoices so that we make sure not to miss any. Our next step is creating the invoices.

Creating Invoices

The time has been entered and and we have created a report for unbilled time, so now we're ready to start creating our invoices. From the Home Page choose *Create Invoices*. When the invoice comes up, the first thing that you are going to do is find the **Customer:Job** box near the top and click the dropdown menu to select your client from the list.

Figure 10.13 Start Creating an Invoice

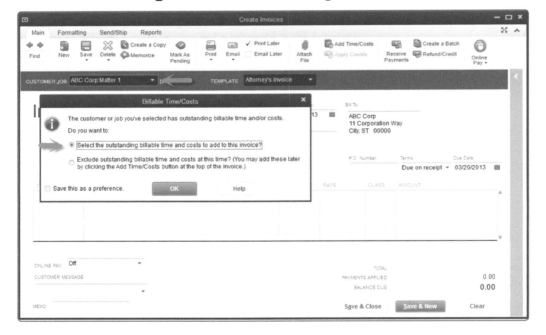

NOTE: QuickBooks does have an autocomplete feature in some text boxes. Click in the box and start typing the first few letters of the client, and QuickBooks will start narrowing the list for you.

After you choose the client, a pop-up box will appear if you have unbilled time/costs for the client (see Figure 10.13). If you do not see the box, check the client name to make sure that you chose the correct one. If the box still doesn't pop up, you might have to double check that the time was assigned to the correct client. This is where using the unbilled time report is handy. You only see the clients that you need to bill, and that cuts down on confusion.

Choose the option *Select the outstanding billable time and costs to add to this invoice?* and then click *OK.*

The Choose Billable Time and Costs box will appear, and you will see all the time you have available to bill your client (see Figure 10.14). Click the *Select All* button to add all of the time, or you can select particular time entries, and leave others unchecked. If you do this, the unchecked entries will stay as unbilled and continue to display in your unbilled time report until they are billed.

Figure 10.14 Choose Billable Time and Costs

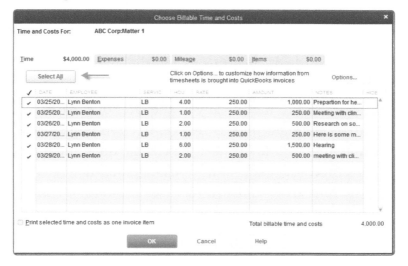

You should also click the *Expenses* and *Items* tabs to see if they have any other charges to add to the bill (see Figure 10.15). Click the *Select*

All button to add all of the expenses, or you can select particular expenses, and leave others unchecked.

Figure 10.15 Checking the Expenses and Items Tabs

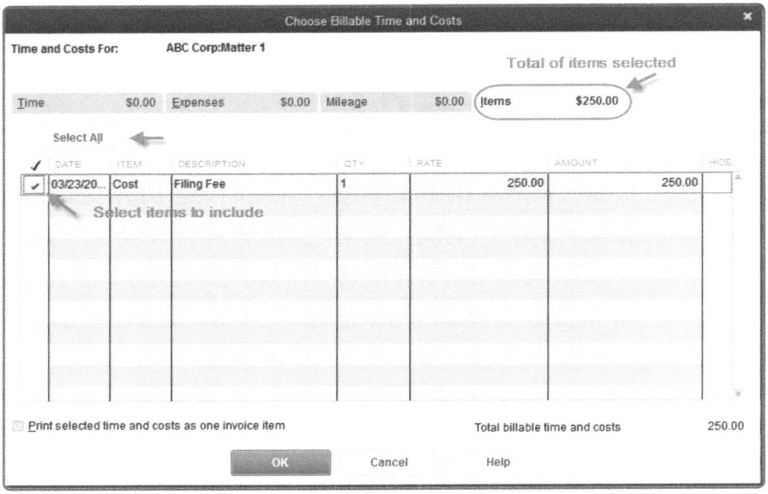

When you have finished, click *OK* to add the items to the invoice.

Once the time is transferred to your invoice, you can modify or add to the invoice. If you want to modify any of the rates or the descriptions, go ahead and do that now right on the invoice. Keep in mind, though, when you change something on the invoice, the change does not appear on the existing timesheet record. If you want to change the time record you will need to go to the time entry and edit that (see Lesson 7 for time tracking).

Unbilled Cost

Before printing invoices, I find that it is a good idea to run the Unbilled Cost Report to make sure I didn't leave any costs out during the billing process. To do this, go to the Main Menu and choose ***Reports***. Then choose ***Jobs, Time & Mileage*** and ***Unbilled Cost by Job*** (see Figure 10.16).

Figure 10.16 Unbilled Costs by Job

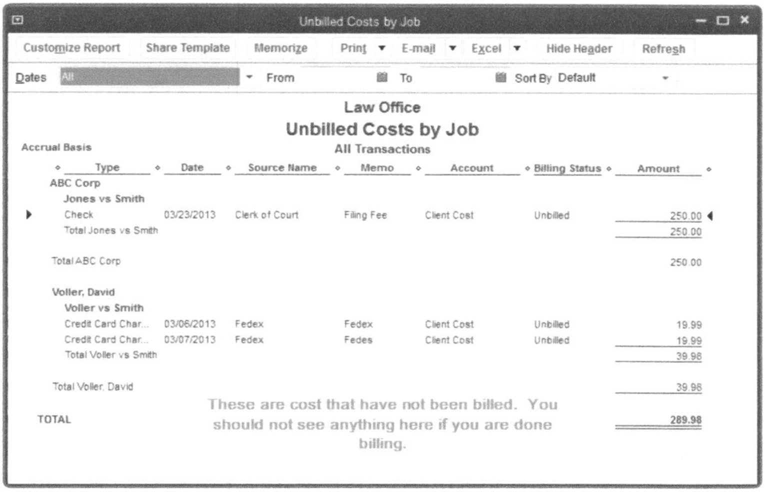
Unbilled Costs by Job

Customize Report | Share Template | Memorize | Print | E-mail | Excel | Hide Header | Refresh

Dates All | From | To | Sort By Default

Law Office
Unbilled Costs by Job
Accrual Basis — All Transactions

Type	Date	Source Name	Memo	Account	Billing Status	Amount
ABC Corp						
Jones vs Smith						
Check	03/23/2013	Clerk of Court	Filing Fee	Client Cost	Unbilled	250.00
Total Jones vs Smith						250.00
Total ABC Corp						250.00
Voller, David						
Voller vs Smith						
Credit Card Char...	03/06/2013	Fedex	Fedex	Client Cost	Unbilled	19.99
Credit Card Char...	03/07/2013	Fedex	Fedes	Client Cost	Unbilled	19.99
Total Voller vs Smith						39.98
Total Voller, David						39.98
TOTAL						289.98

These are cost that have not been billed. You should not see anything here if you are done billing.

When this report is displayed, you should not see anything on it if you have finished with your billing. If you do see something on it, you will need to go back to the original invoice and add these costs. Once you are finished, you are ready to print or e-mail the invoice.

Printing Invoices

You can print the invoice now or wait and print all of the invoices at once. To print or e-mail now, just click the ***Print*** or ***Email*** box at the top of the invoice. To save and print (or e-mail) all of your invoices at one time, make sure the ***Print Later*** (or ***Email Later***) box is selected (see Figure 10.17).

Figure 10.17 Printing Invoices

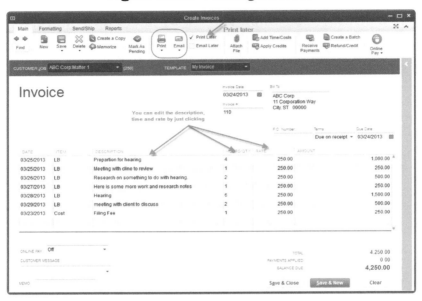

Later, when you are ready to print all of them, click *File*, *Print Forms*, and *Print Invoices*.

Billing Reports

Once invoicing is done, lawyers often ask me if there is a way to generate a report to see what was billed and by whom. Because we set up our items by lawyer way back in Lesson 4, we have a couple of options for generating a report that will give us that information: the **Sales by Item Detail** and **Sales By Item Summary** reports.

From the Main Menu, click *Reports*. Choose *Sales* and then *Sales by Item Summary* or *Sales by Item Detail*.

What we are doing is looking at the service item that is customized with the lawyer's initials (back when we created these in Lesson 4.) As long as everyone uses his or her own items when tracking time, this report will give you a summary or detailed breakdown of the income generated for each lawyer.

You can customize these reports by clicking the **Customize** button and then **Memorize** when you have finished. Figure 10.18 has examples of these reports.

Figure 10.18 Sales by Item Summary and Sales by Item Detail Reports

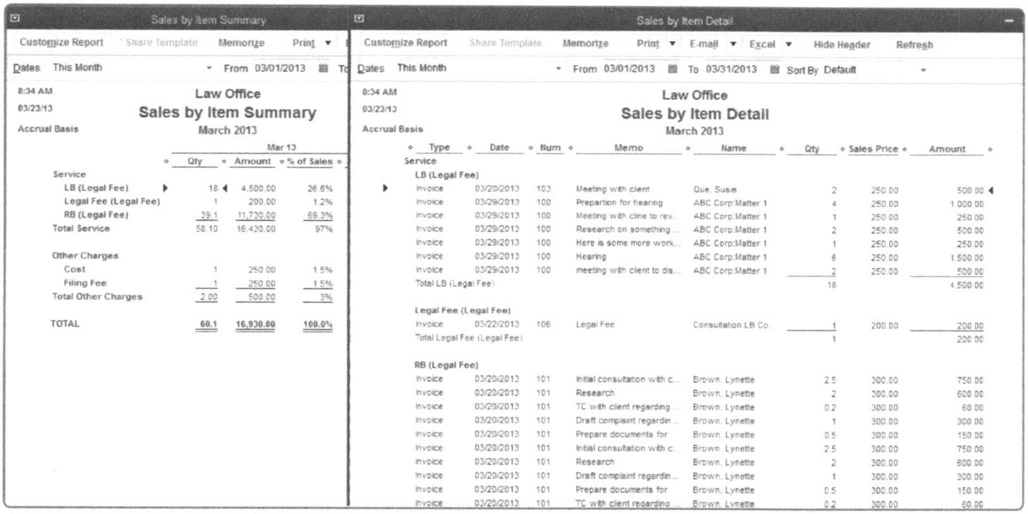

Success! We have completed our billing, and it is time for that break. Soon our money will begin coming in, and we will need to receive it and apply it to each client's account. That is what we are going to cover next.

Receiving Payments

When you receive a payment from a client, you will want to apply it to their account. In QuickBooks, this is called receiving a payment (see Figure 11.1). When you use this feature, QuickBooks will apply the payment to the client's account and also allow you to choose how the payment is applied to an invoice or charge. From the Home Page click **Receive Payments**.

Caution: THIS IS NOT HOW YOU RECEIVE A PAYMENT FOR TRUST ACCOUNT DEPOSITS.

Figure 11.1 Receive Payments

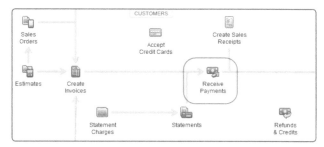

Figure 11.2 shows the Customer Payment window. Choose the client from the ***Received From*** list. If you are using Jobs, it is important to select the Job associated with the client here so the payment is applied to the right client matter. Enter the date of the payment, the amount paid, the type of payment, and a check number or reference number. The type of payment could be cash, check, wire transfer, or credit card.

Figure 11.2 Customer Payment

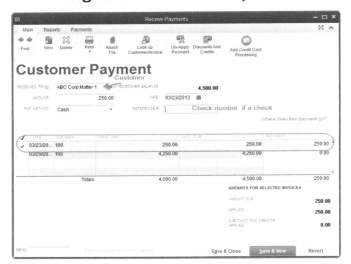

The client may owe $4,500 but only pay $250. The bottom half of the window shows how QuickBooks applies a payment. Although Quick-Books tries its best to apply the payment to the correct invoice, you might need to adjust this. Click the check mark next to a date to uncheck it, and then check the correct date to make the adjustment.

It is important that the payments are applied to the invoices or statement charges. When you are creating profit-and-loss reports based on cash, QuickBooks will only count the money that is applied to an invoice as Income. So make sure that all payments are applied to an invoice to keep everything working right.

> **NOTE:** If you accept credit cards, you may want to look into Intuit's Merchant Service or Payment Network. These services allow you to process credit cards right inside of QuickBooks. The rates are very competitive and, even better, you don't have to sign any long-term contracts. For me, the more I can do in QuickBooks, the better; it means fewer steps to get the job done.

When you are finished, click **Save & Close** or **Save & New** to receive more payments. But wait, we're not quite done yet.

Depositing Money

When you have finished receiving payments, the next step is depositing them into a bank account. By default, QuickBooks holds all received payments in an account called undeposited funds. Think of this account like your real-life bank bag. Clients come in and pay you throughout the day; you receive the payments and credit their account. Later you physically go to the bank to make a deposit. That bank bag is the undeposited funds account.

When you are ready to deposit the money, go to the Home Page and click **Record Deposits**. A window will appear showing the payments you received since your last deposit. Click **Select All** and then click **OK** (see Figure 11.3).

Figure 11.3 Payments to Deposit

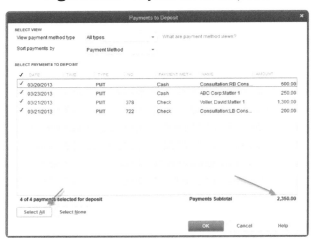

Next, the deposit window appears (see Figure 11.4). To add the deposits to a bank account, choose the bank account and enter the date you are making the deposit. Click **Save & Close** if you are finished or **Save & New** to make a deposit to another account.

Figure 11.4 The Deposit Window

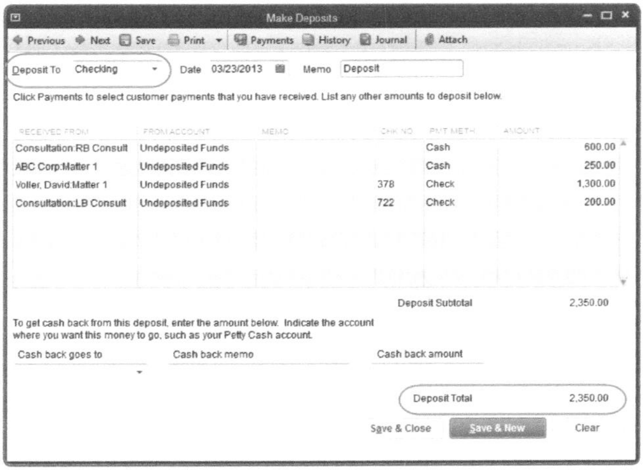

QuickBooks will allow you to print a deposit slip that you can use when you physically take the money to the bank. This can be a time saver, especially if you have a good number of checks to deposit. To do this, you will have to order deposit slips that your bank will accept. You can order preprinted deposit slips from QuickBooks, your bank, or an online source. I use www.checksforless.com because they have great pricing.

You can also print a deposit summary to save with the copies of checks if you would like (see Figure 11.5). Click Save & Close if you are finished or Save & New to make another deposit.

Figure 11.5 Printing a Deposit Summary

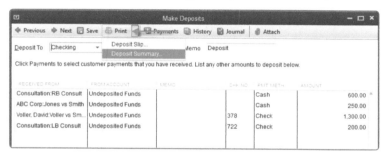

Now we have basically completed the circle: setting up clients, recording time, billing for the time, receiving the payments, and depositing the payments into the bank. Next, I want to show you how to generate reports to see how your firm is doing.

Lesson 12

Reporting on Clients

Some of the most frequently asked questions that I get from new users to QuickBooks are:

- How much do my clients owe me?
- Who has not paid?
- Where's the money?

If these are questions you are asking yourself, you can easily find out by generating a few reports.

Accounts Receivable

First we will prepare a report to answer the question *How much do my clients owe me?* From the Main Menu, click **Reports** and choose **Customers & Receivables**. You will see you have several options (see Figure 12.1). Choose **Customer Balance Summary**.

Figure 12.1 Accounts Receivable Reports

A/R Aging Summary
A/R Aging Detail
Customer Balance Summary
Customer Balance Detail
Open Invoices
Collections Report

This report shows you the total each client owes you. A convenient feature in QuickBooks is the Quick Zoom option that you will see in reports. If you double click the total for customer ABC Corp, it will show you a breakdown of all the activity for that client as shown on the right of Figure 12.2.

Figure 12.2 Summary Report

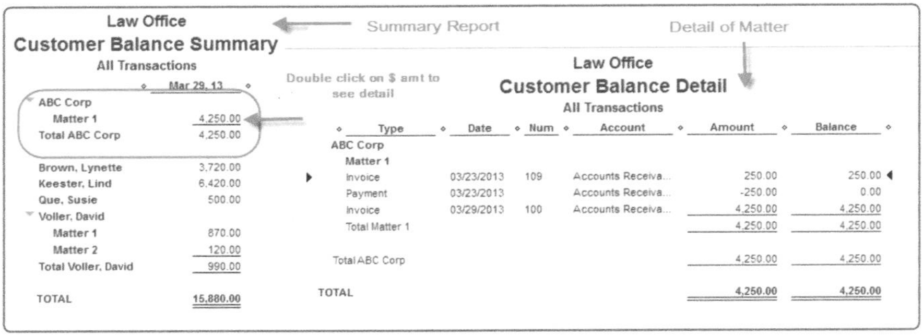

Law Office
Customer Balance Summary
All Transactions

	Mar 29, 13
ABC Corp	
Matter 1	4,250.00
Total ABC Corp	4,250.00
Brown, Lynette	3,720.00
Keester, Lind	6,420.00
Que, Susie	500.00
Voller, David	
Matter 1	870.00
Matter 2	120.00
Total Voller, David	990.00
TOTAL	15,880.00

Law Office
Customer Balance Detail
All Transactions

Type	Date	Num	Account	Amount	Balance
ABC Corp					
Matter 1					
Invoice	03/23/2013	109	Accounts Receiva...	250.00	250.00
Payment	03/23/2013		Accounts Receiva...	-250.00	0.00
Invoice	03/29/2013	100	Accounts Receiva...	4,250.00	4,250.00
Total Matter 1				4,250.00	4,250.00
Total ABC Corp				4,250.00	4,250.00
TOTAL				4,250.00	4,250.00

Remember you can customize and memorize these reports (see Lesson 9).

Another very important report, **Open Invoices**, shows who owes you money (Figure 12.3). You can double click the amount and view the invoice if you want to see the details of the balance. You can view this report by choosing ***Reports*** from the Main Menu, and then ***Customers & Receivables*** and ***Open Invoices***.

Figure 12.3 Open Invoices

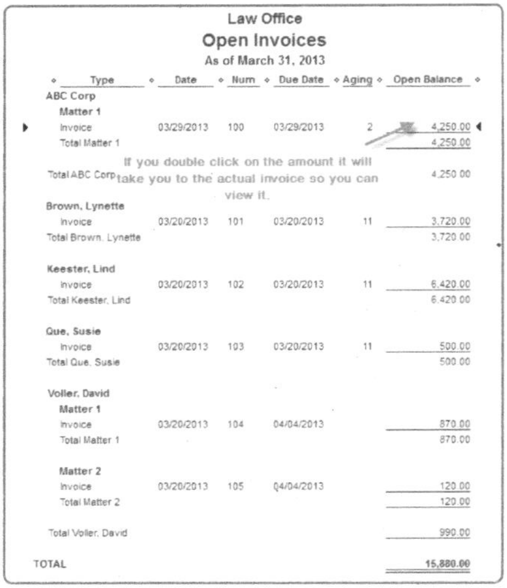

Law Office
Open Invoices
As of March 31, 2013

Type	Date	Num	Due Date	Aging	Open Balance
ABC Corp					
Matter 1					
Invoice	03/29/2013	100	03/29/2013	2	4,250.00
Total Matter 1					4,250.00
Total ABC Corp					4,250.00
Brown, Lynette					
Invoice	03/20/2013	101	03/20/2013	11	3,720.00
Total Brown, Lynette					3,720.00
Keester, Lind					
Invoice	03/20/2013	102	03/20/2013	11	6,420.00
Total Keester, Lind					6,420.00
Que, Susie					
Invoice	03/20/2013	103	03/20/2013	11	500.00
Total Que, Susie					500.00
Voller, David					
Matter 1					
Invoice	03/20/2013	104	04/04/2013		870.00
Total Matter 1					870.00
Matter 2					
Invoice	03/20/2013	105	04/04/2013		120.00
Total Matter 2					120.00
Total Voller, David					990.00
TOTAL					15,880.00

Billing by Client

You can also get billing-by-client summary and detail reports (see Figure 12.4). These reports can be created by the Accrual Basis or the Cash Basis, and they show you how much you have billed your clients and how much you have received from them.

Figure 12.4 Billing (Sales) by Client (Customer)

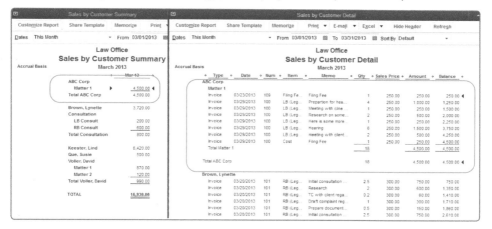

Remember, you can customize any report by clicking the ***Customize*** button and choosing other fields or filtering for one particular client. Once you have done this, Memorize the report so you don't have to customize it each time you want to view it again.

Now it is time to look at how we handle expenses for your business in QuickBooks. We will cover that in our next section.

Handling Expenditures

Up to this point, we have been dealing with the income side of the business. We have watched the money come in by billing for time, invoicing, and receiving payments. But as we all know too well, there is another side to the business—our expenses. This is the side where we watch it go back out just as fast as it comes in.

Before we start working in QuickBooks though, it is important to go back to basic accounting principles to understand exactly what we are working with, so that we can make sure that we are doing it right.

Typically you would want to categorize anything you have to pay for as an expense, but you don't always get to do this. For example, the costs of fixed assets, such as office furniture, new telephones, and another monitor for your desk cannot be expensed right away. Instead, your tax professional will probably depreciate them, and exactly when you can write them off as expenses depends on a number of things including how long they will be in use. Other types of payments, such as those made on loans and credit cards, are really reducing a liability, so they are not really expenses. When you take money out of your business for personal reasons, it is considered a draw or shareholder distribution, depending on your tax structure. So when you are coding expenses, sometimes you will apply them to an expense account and other times you will use a different type of account, such as shareholder distribution or draw.

Costs such as advertising, rent, office supplies, Internet, telephone, dues, entertainment, insurance, and payroll are all expenses. When you are paying for something and you really don't know how to code the expense, there is an account called **Ask my Accountant**. This is a great place to put these types of expenses so your accountant can review them and move them to the right account. It is better to use this account if you are not sure, as guessing can cause headaches later on at tax time.

Ok, I think we are ready. Next we are going to set up our vendors so that we can start making payments.

Vendors

Vendors are people you purchase items or services from. This includes the office supply store, post office, electric company, and many others you give your hard earned money to. In QuickBooks, the Vendor Center is very similar to the Customers and the Employee Center. You have your list of Vendors on the left and information about the vendor on the right. You can enter your vendors ahead of time or you can just enter them as you need to when you write checks.

Setting Up Vendors

To get to the Vendor Center, go to the Main Menu and click **Vendors**. Then choose **Vendor Center**. We are going to add a few vendors here to get started.

To add a new vendor, click the ***New Vendor*** button at the top of the window (see Figure 14.1).

Figure 14.1 New Vendor Button

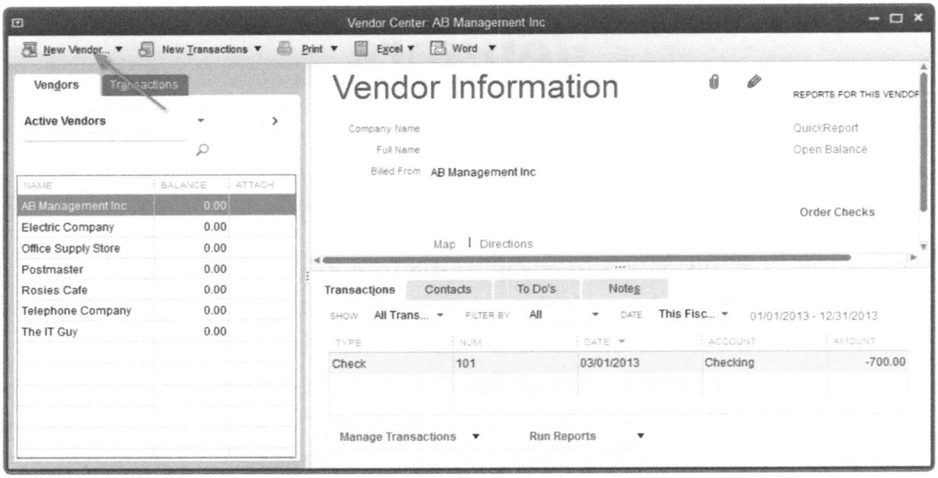

Like the New Customer window, the New Vendor window allows you to add as little or as much information as you want.

Address Info. I would recommend at the very least adding the vendor's address and phone information, which you can do by clicking ***Address Info*** in the column at the left. Other information that you could add is shown in Figure 14.2, including fax, main e-mail, and so on. If you are going to print a check directly from QuickBooks, the **Billed From** field is what will show up on the printed checks. If you are using windowed envelopes to mail payments, adding the address information here is a time saver.

Figure 14.2 Vendor's Address Information

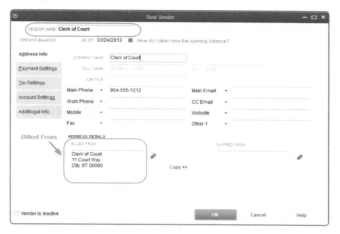

Payment Settings. The second option in the left-hand column (see Figure 14.3) allows you to store information such as your account number and terms. You can also customize how the payee name appears on the check.

Figure 14.3 Payment Settings

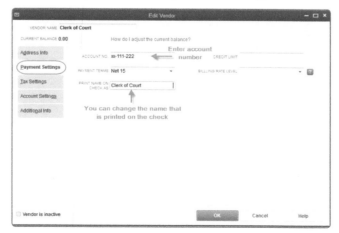

Tax Settings. The next option on the left is Tax Settings. If you will need to issue a 1099 to this vendor, check the ***Vendor eligible for 1099*** box and enter their Tax ID number in the ***Vendor Tax ID*** box (see Figure 14.4). (There is more about 1099 vendors later in this section.)

Figure 14.4 Tax Setting

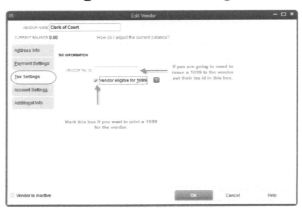

Account Settings. The next option on the left lets you choose the default account that expenses paid to the vendor are applied to (see Figure 14.5). You can change this if needed on the check.

Figure 14.5 Account Settings

Additional Info. Finally, the Additional Info option allows you to set up categories and create custom fields to store information. When you set up categories for your vendors you will be able to get reports by vendor type (see Figure 14.6). Let's say, for example, you wanted to know who all your office supply vendors are or maybe you have several courier services. You could set up a category for each of these.

Figure 14.6 Additional Info

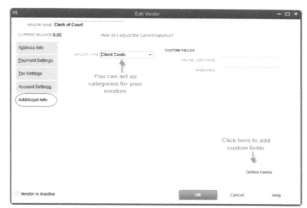

Defining Fields. Defining fields is easy. Click the *Define Fields* button and you will then see the Set up Custom Fields for Names window (see Figure 14.7).

Figure 14.7 Set up Custom Fields for Name

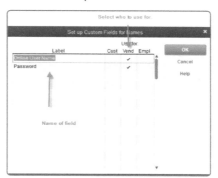

Here you can set up fields and choose whether you want each one to appear on the Customers, Vendors, or Employees window. I love this feature because many of my vendors are online, so now I can store my user names and passwords here.

When you are finished, click **OK**. You can take a moment here and add a few more Vendors into QuickBooks to get the hang of it.

Setting Up 1099 Vendors

What is a 1099? It is a form that the IRS requires you to complete at the end of the year to report payments for services of more than $600. You only need to prepare 1099s for payments made to unincorporated companies or individuals. For example if you have a cleaning lady, a courier, repair guy, or subcontractor who is not incorporated you will need to issue them a 1099 for their services.

At the time of the printing, payments to corporations are exempt from the 1099 rules; however, an exception applies to payments for legal services. If you pay a lawyer or law firm more than $600 for legal services during a calendar year, you also need to prepare a 1099 form for them. For example, when you split fees or work with co-counsel, you need to issue a 1099. Because tax law changes, I recommend downloading the instructions for how and when to report a 1099-Misc form at http://www.irs.gov/pub/irs-pdf/i1099msc.pdf.

QuickBooks will track the amount you spend with your vendor and allow you to print a 1099-Misc form.

Remember from earlier, if you need to set up a 1099 vendor, you first add (or edit) the vendor (see Figure 14.8). Then, from the lefthand column, select *Tax Settings*. Input the Vendor Tax ID number and check the box *Vendor eligible for 1099*.

Figure 14.8 Adding or Editing a Vendor

Paying Vendors

We have now input our vendors into QuickBooks, so now on to the depressing part—writing checks. Creating and printing checks is easy in QuickBooks. Regardless of how you will physically create a check, you will need to enter the information into QuickBooks first. Then at the end, you can decide if you want to handwrite your checks or let QuickBooks print them for you.

From the Home Page, click ***Write Checks***. Next you will see the Write Checks screen (see Figure 14.9). All you have to do here is choose the bank account you are using, enter the date, the payee, the amount, and a memo.

Figure 14.9 Write Checks

Figure 14.10 shows two tabs beneath the check—Expenses and Items. Items are used for tracking costs, like postage and copies that you will later bill your clients for (I will show you how to handle these later in the lesson).

Figure 14.10 Expenses and Items

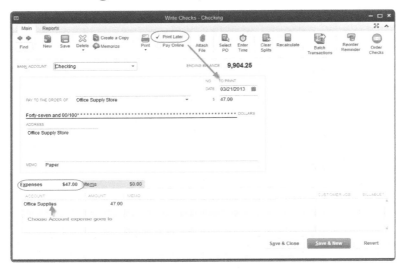

For this example, we are buying paper from the Office Supply Store. In the Expenses tab, choose the expense account (e.g., Office Supplies) from the chart of accounts that the check belongs to.

When you have finished, you can click ***Print***, and then ***Save & New*** if you need to add more, or ***Save & Close*** if you have finished. Go ahead and add a few expenses in now before we move forward.

Printing Checks

Printing checks in QuickBooks is easy and can be a time saver. You can purchase computer checks (sometimes called check stock) from your bank, online, or from an office supply store. I found a place that has check stock at a great price—www.ChecksForLess.com. When ordering your checks, you need to make sure they will work for QuickBooks. There are three basic check styles that QuickBooks will work with: Voucher (check at the top and stub below), Standard (no stub), and Wallet (stub to the left) as shown in Figure 14.11.

Figure 14.11 Check Styles

I have found that the Voucher style, one per page option is the best. This style allows you to send checks to a vendor and retain the bottom stub with the bill you are paying. To save time, I suggest that you staple the stub to your bill instead of taking the time to write "paid" and noting the date and check number on the bill.

You can choose to let QuickBooks print your checks when you are on the Write Checks screen (See Figure 14.10). To print now, click **Print** at the top, or you can choose the **Print Later** option.

If you are going to handwrite the check, you can just enter the check number on this screen. Also, make sure the Print Later option is *not* selected since you are hand writing the check.

When you have finished, click **Save & Close**, or if you want to write other checks, click **Save & New**.

When you create checks and choose the Print Later option, Quick-Books puts those checks in a queue to be printed. When you are ready to print the checks, click **File** from the Main Menu. Then choose **Print Forms** and **Checks**. A dialog box like the one in Figure 14.12 will appear. Choose the **Bank Account** you want to print checks from, verify the **First Check Number** to print on the check, and then select the checks you want to print. If the First Check Number is wrong, you can change it here.

Figure 14.12 Printing Checks

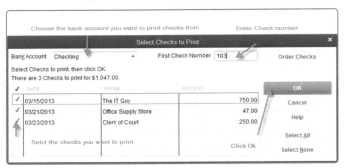

When you click **OK**, you will see another dialog box that allows you to choose the printer and the type of check style you want to print (see Figure 14.13).

Figure 14.13 Choosing the Printer and Check Style

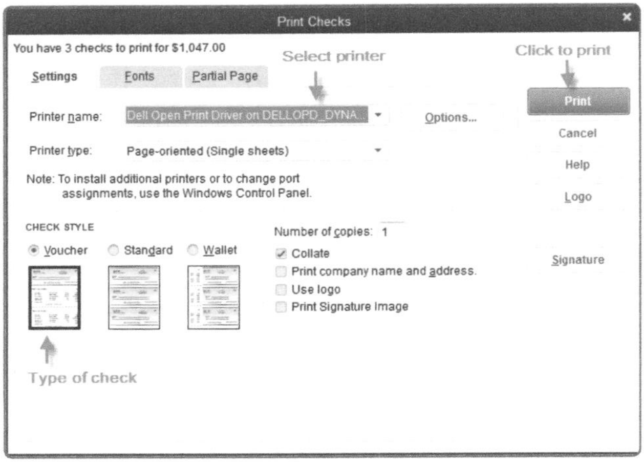

That will cover most of the checks that you will write, but what about the occasion when we write a single check to cover multiple expenses for the same payee? That is where the split transaction comes in.

Split Transactions

Writing a check for multiple expenses is easy. Let's say you want to write one check to pay for a loan. Part of the payment goes to the loan account, and part goes to interest. In the Expense area of the check, you will put the principal loan payment on the first line and add a second line for the interest portion of the payment (see Figure 14.14).

Figure 14.14 Split Transactions

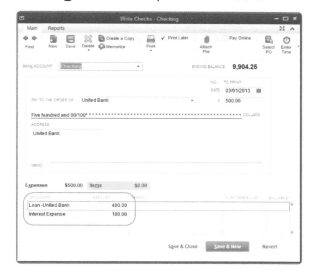

Now you have one check coded to multiple expenses. Click *Save & Close* if you have finished. If you want to create more checks, click *Save & New.*

Paying Client Costs from Your Operating Account

You may use your operating account to write checks for courier fees or FedEx or other expenses you want to bill your clients for later. You start the payment in the same way as other payments: from the top of the Write

Checks screen, you choose the bank account and enter the date, payee, and amount.

Instead of using the **Expenses** tab at the bottom of the check, you use the **Item** tab (see Figure 14.15). Choose *Cost* as the Item, and be sure to enter a *Description*, which will show up on the invoice for the client. Next, choose the client you want to bill in the *Customer:Job* column and make sure you check the box under *Bill?*, so it will be billable.

Figure 14.15 Paying Client Costs from the Operating Account

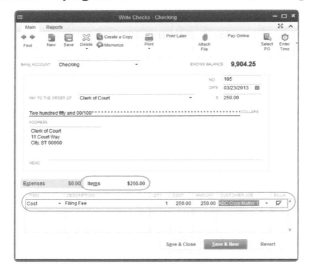

Now that we have written some checks, let's go take a look at the bank account to see how we are doing.

Lesson 15

Your Check Register

The check register in QuickBooks is just like the physical check register that you might keep with a checkbook. Wait . . . do they still have those nowadays, or am I showing my age?

Your QuickBooks check register shows you all the deposits and withdrawals from your account. Every time you write a check or make a deposit, it automatically posts to your check register.

To get to your check register, you can click the **Check Register** icon from your Home Page (see Figure 15.1) or choose **Use Register** from the **Banking** menu item.

You will notice that by default the Register is sorted by date (see Figure 15.2). Each line represents a particular transaction. If you select an item (e.g., check 103 in Figure 15.2) and then choose **Edit Transaction,** you will see the original check.

Figure 15.1
Check Register

Figure 15.2 Check Register

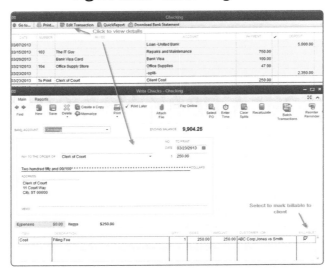

A little tip: if you are not printing out your checks you may find it easier to just enter the checks directly into the check register instead of using the Write Checks window.

Other useful register features are the ability to show just one line of the transaction and the ability to change the color of the register and checks. I find it easier to have my check register the color of my actual checks. This comes in handy when you have multiple bank accounts that you are writing checks out of because you can instantly see if you are in the right account. To do this, click **Edit** from the Main Menu and choose **Change Account Color** (see Figures 15.3a and 15.3b).

Figure 15.3a Changing the Account Color

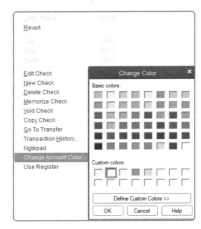

Figure 15.3b After Changing the Account Color

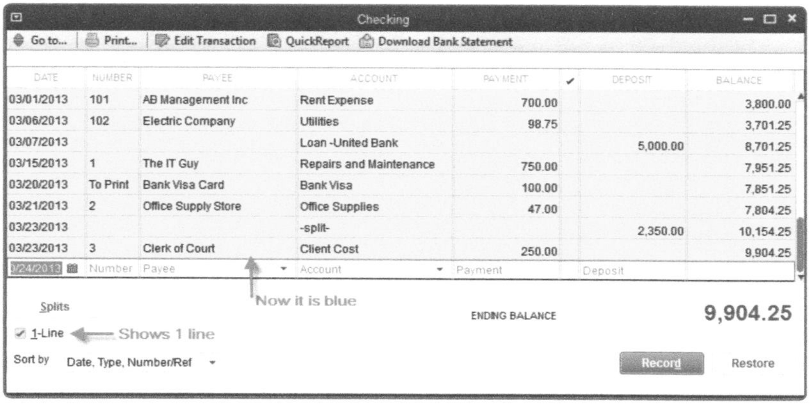

DATE	NUMBER	PAYEE	ACCOUNT	PAYMENT	✔	DEPOSIT	BALANCE
03/01/2013	101	AB Management Inc	Rent Expense	700.00			3,800.00
03/06/2013	102	Electric Company	Utilities	98.75			3,701.25
03/07/2013			Loan -United Bank			5,000.00	8,701.25
03/15/2013	1	The IT Guy	Repairs and Maintenance	750.00			7,951.25
03/20/2013	To Print	Bank Visa Card	Bank Visa	100.00			7,851.25
03/21/2013	2	Office Supply Store	Office Supplies	47.00			7,804.25
03/23/2013			-split-			2,350.00	10,154.25
03/23/2013	3	Clerk of Court	Client Cost	250.00			9,904.25
03/24/2013	Number	Payee	Account	Payment		Deposit	

Now it is blue

Splits

☑ 1-Line ⟵ Shows 1 line

Sort by   Date, Type, Number/Ref ▾

ENDING BALANCE   **9,904.25**

Record   Restore

Recording Credit Card Activity

In addition to your checking account, you may also have a credit card that you use for business expenses. If this is the case, you can track these charges in QuickBooks very easily.

Setting Up Credit Cards

First we will create the account for the credit card. Click **Lists** from the Main Menu and choose **Chart of Accounts**. When the Chart of Accounts list comes up click the **Account** button at the bottom and select **New**. Choose **Credit Card** as the type of account and click **Continue** (see Figure 16.1).

Figure 16.1 Adding a Credit Card Account

Enter the credit card name in the ***Account Name*** and click ***Save & Close*** when you are finished. It is not necessary to fill in all of the other information about the card, so just add enough information to identify it (see Figure 16.2).

Now that we have our account set up, we can add the charges made on this credit card. Because we told QuickBooks it is a credit card, we now have a new button on our Home Page on the lower right corner in the Banking section called **Enter Credit Card Charges** (see Figure 16.3).

Figure 16.2 Fill in Credit Card Name

Figure 16.3 Enter Credit Card Charges

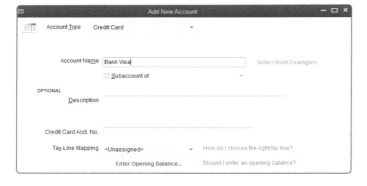

Credit Card Charges

Click on ***Enter Credit Card Charges*** to enter the information about the charge. First, choose the ***Credit Card*** you are using and then enter the vendor you purchased from, the date, and the amount. Like the Write Checks screen, at the bottom are the Expenses and Items tabs. For this example of a purchase from the office supply store, choose the ***Expenses*** tab and enter the ***Account*** and ***Amount*** (see Figure 16.4).

Figure 16.4 Entering the Credit Card Charge Information

If you have other credit card charges that you need to enter, go ahead and enter them now. Next, we will make a payment on our credit card.

Paying Your Credit Card

Because we selected Enter Credit Card Charges to record the expenses paid on the credit card, it is going to be easy to make a payment on the card. All you need to do is write a check, and on the expenses tab, choose the credit card you are paying (see Figure 16.5).

Figure 16.5 Paying the Credit Card

See? That was easy.

Now let's recap how far we have come. It the first section of the book, we covered setting up our clients and billing for our time. We then invoiced our clients and received some money and deposited it into our bank account.

Next, we looked at the expense side by setting up the chart of accounts, adding vendors, and writing checks. We also set up our credit card and made some payments.

You have come a long way! We are almost finished. Only two more lessons to talk about, and they are financial reporting and preparing 1099s. Let's dig right in.

Generating Financial Reports

We have come a long way, but now we need to see how our business is doing. It is time to take a look at a few of the important financial reports that will give us a very clear picture of that.

Cash or Accrual

Like other sections of this book, you need to understand a few accounting concepts before we start generating reports. First, we need to review the differences in accounting methods. There are two methods of accounting reports you can generate in QuickBooks, Accrual and Cash methods reports.

Accrual-based accounting gives you reports based on what you billed your clients (but for which you may or may not have received payment) and bills you owe but have not yet paid.

Cash-based accounting gives you reports based on what you have actually received from your clients and what you have actually spent on expenses. Cash-based reports only account for what has come in and what has gone out at that point in time.

You can set up QuickBooks to run either of these reports by default. From the Main Menu, go to **Edit** and choose **Preferences**. Click the **Reports & Graphs** option in the left-hand column. Select the **Company Preferences** tab. Below **Summary Reports Basis**, choose the method of accounting you want to use by default (see Figure 17.1).

Figure 17.1 Choosing the Default Accounting Method

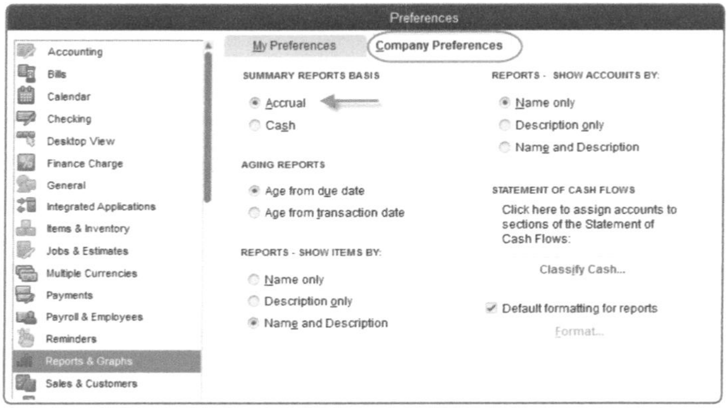

You and perhaps your accountant or tax professional can pick the method that works best for you and your firm. When working with clients, I will generate reports in both cash and accrual methods, depending on what we are looking at, and what information we need.

Reports

There are two main financial statements you will want to learn about: the Balance Sheet and the Profit & Loss statement. In the next section I will explain the differences and step you through producing each.

Balance Sheet Report

A Balance Sheet is a report that summarizes the financial position of your firm. It shows your Assets, Liabilities, and the Equity you have in your business. Remember from basic accounting, Assets – Liabilities = Equity. Said even simpler, a balance sheet lists basically everything you own and everything you owe. It is a snapshot of a particular period of time. For example, if you create a Balance Sheet for the period March 31, 2013 it is going to show you the balances for all your Assets and Liabilities, along with your equity as of that date.

Figure 17.2 Balance Sheet

This is a report that I recommend lawyers generate and take time to go over at the end of the month, after the month-end accounting has been completed. You can print this report (shown in Figure 17.2) by going to the Main Menu and choosing *Reports*, *Company & Financial* and *Balance Sheet Standard*.

By default, this report came up with the Accrual Basis; you can change the accounting basis by clicking on the *Customize* button at the top left and choosing *Cash* or *Accrual* as the accounting method. When you change this report to Cash basis, it will not include Accounts Receivable. Remember that if you customize the report you should Memorize it, so you do not have to recreate it later.

Profit and Loss

The Profit & Loss statement shows your income and expenses. In other words, it answers the question *How much money did your company make (or lose) over a specific period of time?* This report is a checkup for your business, and you can run it any time you are interested in how you are doing.

You can print this report (see Figure 17.3) by going to the Main Menu and choosing ***Reports***, ***Company & Financial***, and ***Profit & Loss Standard***.

You may want to print both methods of accounting for this one because Accrual shows what you billed your clients and Cash shows you what you received from your clients. Notice the difference in the Net Income between the two reports.

Figure 17.3 Profit-and-Loss Statement

Accrual Basis — Law Office — Profit & Loss — March 2013

	Mar 13
Ordinary Income/Expense	
Income	
Legal Fee Income	16,430.00
Reimbursed Client Expense Incom	500.00
Total Income	16,930.00
Expense	
Client Cost	289.98
Interest Expense	100.00
Meals and Entertainment	72.30
Office Supplies	137.00
Rent Expense	700.00
Repairs and Maintenance	750.00
Utilities	98.75
Total Expense	2,148.03
Net Ordinary Income	14,781.97
Net Income	**14,781.97**

Cash Basis — Law Office — Profit & Loss — March 2013

	Mar 13
Ordinary Income/Expense	
Income	
Legal Fee Income	2,100.00
Reimbursed Client Expense Incom	250.00
Total Income	2,350.00
Expense	
Client Cost	289.98
Interest Expense	100.00
Meals and Entertainment	72.30
Office Supplies	137.00
Rent Expense	700.00
Repairs and Maintenance	750.00
Utilities	98.75
Total Expense	2,148.03
Net Ordinary Income	201.97
Net Income	**201.97**

Reports on Income

When you have multiple lawyers and paralegals working in your law firm, you probably want to know how much each has billed and how much money came in from each lawyer's or paralegal's bills. Since we set up our item list with the lawyer's initials this will be easy to create. We will create a Sales by Item report.

To get to this report, go to the Main Menu and click ***Reports***. Choose ***Sales*** and then ***Sales by Item Summary.***

When the report comes up you will see a list of items (people's initials and services) and the amount of sales (billing) for each person (see Figure 17.4). I say *billing* because the accounting method for this report is Accrual Basis.

Figure 17.4 Sales (Billing) by Item (Person)

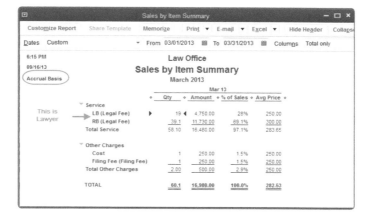

This report lists items that were billed. Our example has two items, one for **LB** and one for **RB**. These are the initials we set up in our item list. If you have more items, they will be listed here.

Let's customize this report. Click the ***Customize Report*** button at the top of the Sales Item Summary Window (see Figure 17.4). Then, click the ***Header/Footer*** tab as shown in Figure 17.5 and enter a report title like ***Billing by Lawyer***.

Figure 17.5 Customizing Billing by Person Report

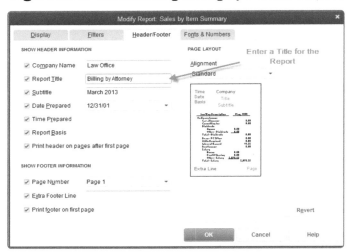

Now that we have a nice report we will Memorize it. Remember earlier (Lesson 9) when I showed you how to create report groups? Let's create a report group called **Billing Reports** and save this and all of your billing reports to this group.

To review how to create a new report group, click **Reports** from the Main Menu and choose **Memorized Report List.** When the list comes up click the **Memorized Report** drop-down menu at the bottom and then select **New Group** (see Figure 17.6).

Figure 17.6 Creating a New Group of Reports

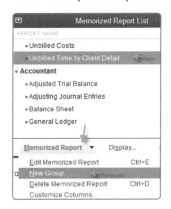

We will name our new group -Billing Reports. Now let's go back to the report we just customized for Billing by Attorney and click the **Memorize** button at the top of the report (see Figure 17.7).

Figure 17.7 Memorizing the Report

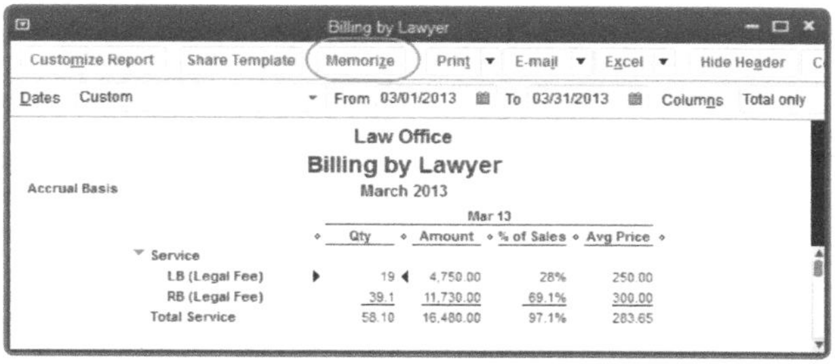

In the Name box enter **Billing by Attorney** and select the **Save in Memorized Report Group** box. Choose **-Billing Reports**. Click **OK** when you have finished (see Figure 17.8).

Now let's create a report that shows us how much money came in during the month by lawyer. This is basically the same report above but we will change the basis to **Cash** and give it a new title called **Receipts by Lawyer** (see Figure 17.9).

Now you can memorize this in the -Billing Reports group.

Figure 17.8 Naming and Filing the Memorized Report

Figure 17.9 Receipts by Lawyer Customized Report

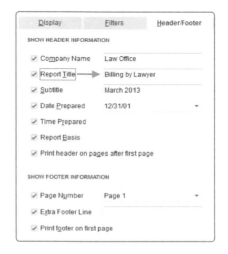

Accounts Receivable

Another good report to create is the Open Invoices Report, which shows you which clients owe you money. Click *Reports* from the Main Menu and choose *Customers & Receivable* and *Open Invoices* (see Figure 17.10).

Figure 17.10 Open Invoices Report

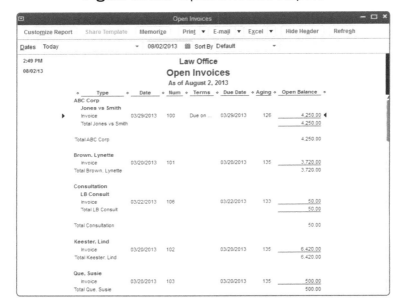

There are a large number of other reports that you can create. Accounts Payable, Profit & Loss by Month, and Customer Sales reports are just a few. While I would love to go through all of the reports here, the scope of this book prevents me from doing so, but you can always check my website at www.attorneystechnology.com/reports-in-qb/ for help in creating some of these reports.

Lesson 18

Preparing 1099s

In January you will need to prepare 1099s and 1096s to send to your vendors and to the IRS. With so many changes in the tax law and reporting requirements, I recommend going to the **irs.gov** website and downloading the Instructions for 1099s. QuickBooks has a built-in feature to help you prepare these forms, and you can submit them online using the E-file service through QuickBooks.

To prepare 1099-MISC you can use the QuickBooks 1099 Wizard. From the Main Menu choose *Vendors,* then *Print/E-file 1099s*, and then *1099 Wizard*. You should see a window similar to Figure 18.1. Click the *Get Started* button at the bottom.

Figure 18.1 The 1099 and 1096 Wizard

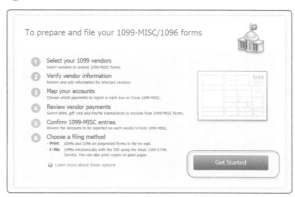

QuickBooks will display all your vendors and show you which ones you have marked as a 1099 vendor (see Figure 18.2). You can review the list and mark additional vendors that are not selected. When you are finished reviewing click the ***Continue*** button at the bottom.

Figure 18.2 Select 1099 Vendors

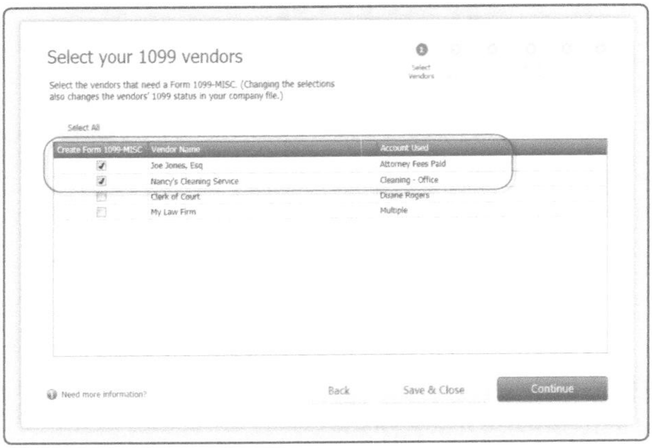

Figure 18.3 shows a listing of all the vendors you have selected and the information needed for the 1099, such as the Taxpayer ID number, name,

Figure 18.3 List of 1099 Vendors

and address. If anything is missing or needs to be changed, you can change it here. QuickBooks will save the changes right from this screen.

Click *Continue* when you have finished.

Now you will assign the expense accounts that you used to pay the vendors to the appropriate 1099 box (see Figure 18.4). For example, rents paid will go to box 1; non-employee compensation for contractors, such as our cleaning lady, will go to box 7. Fees paid to lawyers outside your firm for co-council go to box 14. If you need more help deciding which box to choose click on *Tell me more about the 1099 boxes*. You can also refer to the 1099 instructions publication from the irs.gov website. When you have finished mapping your accounts click *Continue*.

Figure 18.4 Assigning Payments to 1099 Boxes

You can now choose to view the included and excluded payments so you can double-check the amounts (see Figure 18.5). Beginning with the 2011 tax year, the IRS requires you to exclude from Form 1099-MISC any payments you made by credit card, debit card, gift card, or third-party payment network such as PayPal. (These payments are being reported by the card issuers and third-party payment networks on Form 1099-K.)

Click *Continue* when you are finished.

Figure 18.5 Review Included and Excluded Payments

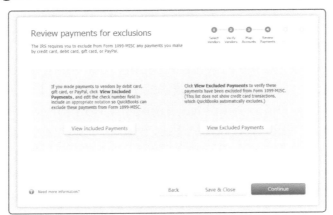

You will now see the Confirm your 1099 entries window as shown in Figure 18.6. Here you will notice a column for unmapped amounts. You want to see 0.00 here. Pay attention to this because it will show you if you paid a vendor and assigned it to an account that you have not mapped to show up on 1099s. For example, let's say you paid the cleaning lady one

Figure 18.6 Confirm Your 1099 Entries

time and coded it to repairs and maintenance instead of cleaning. If you see a mistake, you can click the back button and fix it. Click ***Continue*** once you're sure everything is correct.

You are now ready to print your 1099s (see Figure 18.7).

Figure 18.7 Printing or E-filing 1099s

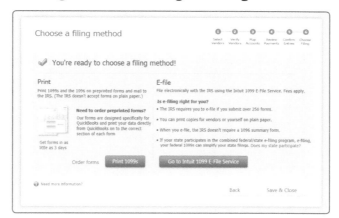

QuickBooks offers an E-File service that you can participate in. Two advantages are that you don't have to buy preprinted forms and you can submit the forms electronically. Click ***Go to Intuit 1099 E-File Service*** to learn more.

Other Important Stuff

Whew! We made it. Through this book we have learned all the basics you need to get started with QuickBooks. Even if you have never used the software before, you now know enough to run your business, bill your clients, pay your expenses, and run reports to see how you are doing.

But as you have moved through the program, I am sure you have noticed that there is plenty more to learn. As I tell all my clients, get the basics down so they become second nature, and then you can start to branch out. That being said, there are a few final thoughts that I want to leave you with.

Trust Accounting

This is a biggie. Probably one of the things that keeps lawyers up at night is not knowing if they have adequate trust account records. Yes, Quick-Books can handle trust accounting if you set it up right. I have a very simple method of tracking what comes in and what goes out of a trust account. When you do things correctly, you can easily get the reports you need to help you stay in compliance with bar regulations.

When you are using the trust account you will set up two accounts. A Bank Account called Trust and a Current Liability Account called Trust Liability. The reason you set up a liability account is because this money is not yours. It's not income and it's not an expense.

Before you deposit monies into the trust account you need to set up subaccounts under the Trust Liability. This way each client's funds are in their own account, and you will be able to view client ledgers and information for just that one client's activity.

Users often make some very common mistakes when working with a trust account: they apply funds paid out of trust to an expense account, and they transfer money directly from Trust to an Operating Account. *Everything* going into and out of the trust account will get applied to the Trust Liability.

The trust accounting in QuickBooks is beyond the scope of this book but you can go to www.AttorneysTechnology.com/trust-accounting-tips/ to see some resources on the best way to set up and maintain a trust account. I have written a book called *Trust Accounting Using QuickBooks* (www.AttorneysTechnology.com/trust-accounting/) that covers the entire process, beginning to end. If you have a trust account, you need to know which reports are required so you can stay in compliance.

Back Up Your Data

"Oh my goodness! My data is gone!" I have heard this more than a few times. Backing up your data can be a lifesaver, and it is easy to do in QuickBooks. You can back up QuickBooks to your own online service or back it up to a simple flash drive. My biggest recommendation is making sure you are backing up and making sure you know how to get to it once it is backed up. And make sure you test your backups more than once a year.

It is easy to back up in QuickBooks. Simply click ***File*** from the Main Menu and choose ***Back up***. You will be guided through screens that will let you pick the location. You can also visit my blog at http://attorneys technology.com/schedule-back-up-in-quickbooks/ to see step-by-step instructions about how to set up an automatic backup.

Which Version of QuickBooks Do You Choose?

Several versions of QuickBooks are available at the time of this book's publication. They include QuickBooks Online, QuickBooks for Mac, QuickBooks Pro, QuickBooks Premier, and QuickBooks Enterprise. Choosing the right one for your business can be confusing, but the following questions may help you decide which version to get.

Do you need more than three people to have access to QuickBooks? QuickBooks Pro is out because it only allows three simultaneous users at a time. You will want to choose from QuickBooks Premier, Enterprise, or Online.

If you need more than five people to have simultaneous access to your QuickBooks company data file, then you will have to go with the Enterprise edition because it allows up to thirty users. This edition costs substantially more, but, when a new version is released you automatically receive the new upgrade. At the time of this book printing, the Enterprise edition also offers a maintenance plan that provides free technical support via chat or phone for one year. Enterprise edition is definitely worth the cost if you have multiple people who need access to QuickBooks.

When thinking of users that need access to the program, you may want to think about what they need to do. For example, many law firms just need their lawyers to be able to enter time in QuickBooks. If this is the case, you may not need to buy full versions of QuickBooks for everyone. There are also quite a few add-on products that allow you to enter time which then gets imported into QuickBooks for billing. **Eztime** (www.ezwebtime.com) is one of these products, and it's very inexpensive. However, if you are using practice management software that includes time and billing, the time can usually be imported into QuickBooks easily, so there's no need to buy Eztime or any other add-on product.

Do you need access to the QuickBooks file anywhere anytime? If so, you might consider using **QuickBooks Online** (http://quickbooks.intuit. com/online/). The basic cost starts at about $12.95 per month, not including payroll and some other features. If you need more than one person besides your accountant to have access to the file, you will need to upgrade to Online Plus which starts around $39.95 a month, not including payroll. This is not my favorite choice because I find it a bit cumbersome when it comes to tracking time and billing clients. Compared to the desktop versions, it can be more expensive and many agree that it is not the easiest to use. In addition, there are some things you can't do in the online version, like set price levels for clients. So if you have clients you bill at different rates, the online version is out.

Speaking of price levels, do you want the ability to set up different rates for individual clients? This is a biggie. If you do, then you will have to go with the Premier or Enterprise versions. This not only allows you to set up rates for clients but rates for your employees. While it usually costs about $100 more per license than QuickBooks Pro, if you need price levels, it is well worth the extra cost upfront because it will save time every time you do billing.

Do you track time? If so, and you want to bill your clients using the invoice method, QuickBooks Premier Edition is perfect for this. It allows you to see unbilled time and expenses on one screen and bill for them very easily.

Are you just starting your law practice and still unsure of which version to get? I would recommend the QuickBooks Premier Edition. It is better to have the features available up front, so if you discover you need them, you have them ready to go. Price levels and the ability to bill your time in one screen when using the invoice method are significant advantages, and the cost difference is minimal when you look at the big picture.

Appendix B

Setup Checklist

You can use this as a guide to help you get the items together that you need to get started using QuickBooks.

Company Info

- The company's legal name, address, and the type of entity
- Federal, state, and local identification numbers
- Fiscal year-end date
- Type of income tax form filed
- The names of QuickBooks users and the QuickBooks areas to which they should have access

Lists

- List of customers, including their addresses and contact information
- List of vendors, including their addresses and contact information. If 1099 vendor you will also need Tax ID.
- Trial balance as of the start date. You may want to consult with your accountant for this.

Payroll

- Payroll start date
- State and federal Tax IDs
- Types of compensation paid (e.g., hourly wages, salaries, commissions)
- Types of deductions withheld (e.g., health or life insurance paid by employees)
- Names, addresses, Social Security numbers and filing status for each employee
- Summaries of employee payroll amounts from the beginning of the current calendar year to the start date

Accounts Receivable/Sales

- Invoices or statement charges and credit memos made between the start date and setup date
- Payments received and refunds made between the start date and setup date

Other Transactions

- Record of checks written between the start date and setup date
- Record of other deposits made between the start date and setup date
- Credit card statements showing charges and payments made between the start date and setup date

Sample Item List

This first sample is of a list of items using lawyer's initials and sub-items. The use of sub items lets you get a little more detail into what you spend most of your time on. Of course, replace my initials (LB) with your own.

LB. This is the main item and below are the sub items for LB.

LB: Admin Time

LB: Case Management

LB: Court Appearance

LB: Meetings

LB: Legal Research

LB: Legal Writing

LB: No Charge

LB: ProBono

LB: Telephone

RB. This is the main item and below are the sub items for RB.

RB: Admin Time

RB: Case Management

RB: Court Appearance

RB: Meetings

RB: Legal Research

RB: Legal Writing

RB: No Charge

RB: ProBono

RB: Telephone

This next list is a sample list of items you may want to use instead of using initials.

Beg Balance

Case Management

Court Appearance

Legal Writing

Legal Research

Meetings

No Charge

ProBono

Settlements

Telephone

Travel

Reimbursable Expenses

Reimbursable Expenses: Filing & Court Fees

Reimbursable Expenses: Mileage

Reimbursable Expenses: Overnight Mail

Reimbursable Expenses: Printing

Unbillable Time

Unbillable Time: Accounting
Unbillable Time: Brochure Dev
Unbillable Time: Client Contract
Unbillable Time: Marketing
Unbillable Time: Meetings
Unbillable Time: Personnel
Unbillable Time: Proposal Dev
Unbillable Time: Sick Leave
Unbillable Time: Training
Unbillable Time: Vacation

Sample Small Law Firm
Chart of Accounts

Account	Type
Operating	Bank
Trust Account	Bank
Accounts Receivable	Accounts Receivable
Undeposited Funds	Other Current Asset
Accumulated Depreciation	Fixed Asset
Furniture and Equipment	Fixed Asset
Security Deposits Asset	Other Asset
Client Trust Liability	Other Current Liability
Client Trust Liability: Firm Funds	Other Current Liability
Client Trust Liability: IOLTA Interest	Other Current Liability
Loan: Big City Bank	Other Current Liability
Payroll Liabilities	Other Current Liability
Capital Stock	Equity
Retained Earnings	Equity
Shareholder Distributions	Equity
Legal Fee Income	Income

Reimbursed Client Expenses Income	Income
Accounting Fees	Expense
Advertising and Promotion	Expense
Automobile Expense	Expense
Bank and Credit Card Service Charges	Expense
Client Cost	Expense
Computer and Internet Expenses	Expense
Continuing Legal Education	Expense
Depreciation Expense	Expense
Dues and Subscriptions	Expense
Insurance Expense	Expense
Insurance Expense: Disability	Expense
Insurance Expense: Professional Liability	Expense
Interest Expense	Expense
Legal Library	Expense
Meals and Entertainment	Expense
Office Supplies	Expense
Payroll Expenses	Expense
Postage and Delivery	Expense
Professional Fees	Expense
Rent Expense	Expense
Repairs and Maintenance	Expense
Research Services	Expense
Telephone Expense	Expense
Travel Expense	Expense
Utilities	Expense
Ask My Accountant	Other Expense

Index

LinkedIn in One Hour for Lawyers, Second Edition
By Dennis Kennedy and Allison C. Shields
Product Code: 5110773 • **LPM Price:** $39.95 • **Regular Price:** $49.95

Since the first edition of LinkedIn in One Hour for Lawyers was published, LinkedIn has added almost 100 million users, and more and more lawyers are using the platform on a regular basis. Now, this bestselling ABA book has been fully revised and updated to reflect significant changes to LinkedIn's layout and functionality made through 2013. LinkedIn in One Hour for Lawyers, Second Edition, will help lawyers make the most of their online professional networking. In just one hour, you will learn to:

- Set up a LinkedIn® account
- Create a robust, dynamic profile--and take advantage of new multimedia options
- Build your connections
- Get up to speed on new features such as Endorsements, Influencers, Contacts, and Channels
- Enhance your Company Page with new functionality
- Use search tools to enhance your network
- Monitor your network with ease
- Optimize your settings for privacy concerns
- Use LinkedIn® effectively in the hiring process
- Develop a LinkedIn strategy to grow your legal network

Blogging in One Hour for Lawyers
By Ernie Svenson
Product Code: 5110744 • **LPM Price:** $24.95 • **Regular Price:** $39.95

Until a few years ago, only the largest firms could afford to engage an audience of millions. Now, lawyers in any size firm can reach a global audience at little to no cost—all because of blogs. An effective blog can help you promote your practice, become more "findable" online, and take charge of how you are perceived by clients, journalists and anyone who uses the Internet. Blogging in One Hour for Lawyers will show you how to create, maintain, and improve a legal blog—and gain new business opportunities along the way. In just one hour, you will learn to:

- Set up a blog quickly and easily
- Write blog posts that will attract clients
- Choose from various hosting options like Blogger, TypePad, and WordPress
- Make your blog friendly to search engines, increasing your ranking
- Tweak the design of your blog by adding customized banners and colors
- Easily send notice of your blog posts to Facebook and Twitter
- Monitor your blog's traffic with Google Analytics and other tools
- Avoid ethics problems that may result from having a legal blog

The Electronic Evidence and Discovery Handbook: Forms, Checklists, and Guidelines
By Sharon D. Nelson, Bruce A. Olson, and John W. Simek
Product Code: 5110569 • **LPM Price:** $99.95 • **Regular Price:** $129.95

The use of electronic evidence has increased dramatically over the past few years, but many lawyers still struggle with the complexities of electronic discovery. This substantial book provides lawyers with the templates they need to frame their discovery requests and provides helpful advice on what they can subpoena. In addition to the ready-made forms, the authors also supply explanations to bring you up to speed on the electronic discovery field. The accompanying CD-ROM features over 70 forms, including, Motions for Protective Orders, Preservation and Spoliation Documents, Motions to Compel, Electronic Evidence Protocol Agreements, Requests for Production, Internet Services Agreements, and more. Also included is a full electronic evidence case digest with over 300 cases detailed!

Facebook® in One Hour for Lawyers
By Dennis Kennedy and Allison C. Shields
Product Code: 5110745 • **LPM Price:** $24.95 • **Regular Price:** $39.95

With a few simple steps, lawyers can use Facebook® to market their services, grow their practices, and expand their legal network—all by using the same methods they already use to communicate with friends and family. Facebook® in One Hour for Lawyers will show any attorney—from Facebook® novices to advanced users—how to use this powerful tool for both professional and personal purposes.

Android Apps in One Hour for Lawyers
By Daniel J. Siegel
Product Code: 5110754 • **LPM Price:** $19.95 • **Regular Price:** $34.95

Lawyers are already using Android devices to make phone calls, check e-mail, and send text messages. After the addition of several key apps, Android smartphones or tablets can also help run a law practice. From the more than 800,000 apps currently available, Android Apps in One Hour for Lawyers highlights the "best of the best" apps that will allow you to practice law from your mobile device. In just one hour, this book will describe how to buy, install, and update Android apps, and help you:

- Store documents and files in the cloud
- Use security apps to safeguard client data on your phone
- Be organized and productive with apps for to-do lists, calendar, and contacts
- Communicate effectively with calling, text, and e-mail apps
- Create, edit, and organize your documents
- Learn on the go with news, reading, and reference apps
- Download utilities to keep your device running smoothly
- Hit the road with apps for travel
- Have fun with games and social media apps

Virtual Law Practice:
How to Deliver Legal Services Online
By Stephanie L. Kimbro

Product Code: 5110707 • **LPM Price:** $47.95 • **Regular Price:** $79.95

The legal market has recently experienced a dramatic shift as lawyers seek out alternative methods of practicing law and providing more affordable legal services. Virtual law practice is revolutionizing the way the public receives legal services and how legal professionals work with clients. If you are interested in this form of practicing law, *Virtual Law Practice* will help you:

- Responsibly deliver legal services online to your clients
- Successfully set up and operate a virtual law office
- Establish a virtual law practice online through a secure, client-specific portal
- Manage and market your virtual law practice
- Understand state ethics and advisory opinions
- Find more flexibility and work/life balance in the legal profession

Social Media for Lawyers: The Next Frontier
By Carolyn Elefant and Nicole Black

Product Code: 5110710 • **LPM Price:** $47.95 • **Regular Price:** $79.95

The world of legal marketing has changed with the rise of social media sites such as Linkedin, Twitter, and Facebook. Law firms are seeking their companies attention with tweets, videos, blog posts, pictures, and online content. Social media is fast and delivers news at record pace. This book provides you with a practical, goal-centric approach to using social media in your law practice that will enable you to identify social media platforms and tools that fit your practice and implement them easily, efficiently, and ethically.

iPad Apps in One Hour for Lawyers
By Tom Mighell

Product Code: 5110739 • **LPM Price:** $19.95 • **Regular Price:** $34.95

At last count, there were more than 80,000 apps available for the iPad. Finding the best apps often can be an overwhelming, confusing, and frustrating process. iPad Apps in One Hour for Lawyers provides the "best of the best" apps that are essential for any law practice. In just one hour, you will learn about the apps most worthy of your time and attention. This book will describe how to buy, install, and update iPad apps, and help you:

- Find apps to get organized and improve your productivity
- Create, manage, and store documents on your iPad
- Choose the best apps for your law office, including litigation and billing apps
- Find the best news, reading, and reference apps
- Take your iPad on the road with apps for travelers
- Maximize your social networking power
- Have some fun with game and entertainment apps during your relaxation time

Twitter in One Hour for Lawyers
By Jared Correia

Product Code: 5110746 • **LPM Price:** $24.95 • **Regular Price:** $39.95

More lawyers than ever before are using Twitter to network with colleagues, attract clients, market their law firms, and even read the news. But to the uninitiated, Twitter's short messages, or tweets, can seem like they are written in a foreign language. Twitter in One Hour for Lawyers will demystify one of the most important social-media platforms of our time and teach you to tweet like an expert. In just one hour, you will learn to:

- Create a Twitter account and set up your profile
- Read tweets and understand Twitter jargon
- Write tweets—and send them at the appropriate time
- Gain an audience—follow and be followed
- Engage with other Twitters users
- Integrate Twitter into your firm's marketing plan
- Cross-post your tweets with other social media platforms like Facebook and LinkedIn
- Understand the relevant ethics, privacy, and security concerns
- Get the greatest possible return on your Twitter investment
- And much more!

The Lawyer's Essential Guide to Writing
By Marie Buckley

Product Code: 5110726 • **LPM Price:** $47.95 • **Regular Price:** $79.95

This is a readable, concrete guide to contemporary legal writing. Based on Marie Buckley's years of experience coaching lawyers, this book provides a systematic approach to all forms of written communication, from memoranda and briefs to e-mail and blogs. The book sets forth three principles for powerful writing and shows how to apply those principles to develop a clean and confident style.

iPad in One Hour for Lawyers, Second Edition
By Tom Mighell

Product Code: 5110747 • **LPM Price:** $24.95 • **Regular Price:** $39.95

Whether you are a new or a more advanced iPad user, *iPad in One Hour for Lawyers* takes a great deal of the mystery and confusion out of using your iPad. Ideal for lawyers who want to get up to speed swiftly, this book presents the essentials so you don't get bogged down in technical jargon and extraneous features and apps. In just six, short lessons, you'll learn how to:

- Quickly Navigate and Use the iPad User Interface
- Set Up Mail, Calendar, and Contacts
- Create and Use Folders to Multitask and Manage Apps
- Add Files to Your iPad, and Sync Them
- View and Manage Pleadings, Case Law, Contracts, and other Legal Documents
- Use Your iPad to Take Notes and Create Documents
- Use Legal-Specific Apps at Trial or in Doing Research

30-DAY RISK-FREE ORDER FORM

Please print or type. To ship UPS, we must have your street address. If you list a P.O. Box, we will ship by U.S. Mail.

Name

Member ID

Firm/Organization

Street Address

City/State/Zip

Area Code/Phone (In case we have a question about your order)

E-mail

Method of Payment:
☐ Check enclosed, payable to American Bar Association
☐ MasterCard   ☐ Visa   ☐ American Express

Card Number   Expiration Date

Signature Required

MAIL THIS FORM TO:
American Bar Association, Publication Orders
P.O. Box 10892, Chicago, IL 60610

ORDER BY PHONE:
24 hours a day, 7 days a week:
Call 1-800-285-2221 to place a credit card order. We accept Visa, MasterCard, and American Express.

EMAIL ORDERS: orders@americanbar.org
FAX ORDERS: 1-312-988-5568

VISIT OUR WEB SITE: www.ShopABA.org
Allow 7-10 days for regular UPS delivery. Need it sooner? Ask about our overnight delivery options. Call the ABA Service Center at 1-800-285-2221 for more information.

GUARANTEE:
If—for any reason—you are not satisfied with your purchase, you may return it within 30 days of receipt for a refund of the price of the book(s). No questions asked.

Thank You For Your Order.

Join the ABA Law Practice Division today and receive a substantial discount on Division publications!

Product Code:	Description:	Quantity:	Price:	Total Price:
				$
				$
				$
				$
				$

**Shipping/Handling:

$0.00 to $9.99	add $0.00
$10.00 to $49.99	add $6.95
$50.00 to $99.99	add $8.95
$100.00 to $199.99	add $10.95
$200.00 to $499.99	add $13.95

*Tax:
IL residents add 9.25%
DC residents add 6%

Subtotal:	$
*Tax:	$
**Shipping/Handling:	$
Yes, I am an ABA member and would like to join the Law Practice Division today! (Add $50.00)	$
Total:	$